THE SUNSHINE ROAD

THE SUNSHINE ROAD

David & Juneau Chagall

THOMAS NELSON PUBLISHERS

Nashville

Some of the names have been changed herein to protect the privacy of certain individuals and their families.

Copyright © 1988 by David Chagall and Juneau Chagall

Published in Nashville, Tennessee, by Thomas Nelson, Inc. and distributed in Canada by Lawson Falle, Ltd., Cambridge, Ontario.

Printed in the United States of America.

Scripture quotations are from THE NEW KING JAMES VERSION of the Bible. Copyright © 1979, 1980, 1982, Thomas Nelson, Inc., Publishers.

ISBN 0-8407-7623-3

1 2 3 4 5 6—92 91 90 89 88

OUR THANKS TO THE SPIRIT OF TRUTH,
AND TO ED RICHTER,
WHO NEVER KNEW IT WOULD TAKE
TWENTY-FOUR YEARS FOR US TO FIND OUT
WHAT ROMANS 8:28
IS REALLY ALL ABOUT.

Contents

THE SUNSHINE ROAD

1

Making It

The phone rang, shattering an early afternoon calm. I was in the office typing out a manuscript, but I paused to listen as Juneau answered in the living room.

"Just a moment, please," I heard her say and in seconds she stood by the door. "It's New York," she said.

"Who is it?" I asked.

"A woman. She didn't give her name."

Free-lance writers usually don't enjoy being surprised on the phone. Having to shift quickly from the inward-looking writing trance to the sharp wits demanded by business questions often catches us off guard, and over the years I'd agreed to deals I began regretting even before I hung up the receiver. Scouring my mind for which publisher or agent might be calling—and coming up with a big zero—I cradled the phone warily to my ear.

"Hello," I said.

"Hello, David Chagall?"

"Yes."

"This is Christine Imperatyl with the Association of American Publishers in New York. I've got good news for you," she said. "*Diary of a Deaf Mute* has been nominated for this year's National Book Award in fiction."

"Oh," I stammered. "That's . . . that's very exciting."

"We'll let you know as soon as we can after the committee make their final selections. Meanwhile, congratulations on writing one of the five best novels of the year."

"Thank you," I said. "I'm honored and grateful."

She clicked off, and I stood there awhile with the phone in my hand. My mind time-traveled back a dozen years to when I had first written the book, composed over a six-week span of evenings and weekends while I held down a full-time job compiling civil service exams.

Diary of a Deaf Mute had been an experiment in automatic writing. I had surrendered all conscious control to "the spirit" leading my fingers across the typewriter keys. The whole 190-page manuscript was done this way behind a marijuana high, which I smoked to blot out the turmoil of the workaday world, allowing me to enter the floating freedom of creative consciousness.

It was a time when my friends and I were consumed with the passion of "making it," laying our bodies, energies, wives, and families on the altar of success. The fifties doldrums were behind us, the apocalyptic sixties still loomed ahead, and anything offering to help us gain wealth and fame was by definition worth a go. "Don't knock it if you haven't tried it" was our battle cry.

That meant mind-control philosophies, psychic powers, astrology, drugs, protest, rebellion, spirit guides, ESP—in short, the whole glittering grab bag of New Age tools and revolutionary notions promising us whatever our hearts craved. Though we didn't know it then, it was a path that would lead us halfway around the world, produce breakdowns, suicide and murder, and put some of us into the pages of *Who's Who* and others into prisons or an early grave.

Yet—despite the pits, rocks, and thorns—signposts along the way kept leading us toward a beckoning golden warmth, drawing us with tender power that never clamored. And there, at the end of the Sunshine Road, we finally found our questions answered and our joy made complete. But like most of life's journeys aimed at winning the easy way and being Number One, our trip began in ignorance and with innocent first steps.

2

Chasing Rainbows

"God, God, God. What's all this garbage about God?" Dimitri was a composer and Reichian psychology devotee. "God may have been Handel's crutch, but when I sit down to write, God doesn't have a thing to do with it. When I'm functioning right, the music comes easy—when my energies are messed up, it doesn't. It's as simple as that."

We sat at a table in the Gilded Cage, a popular coffee shop off posh Rittenhouse Square in downtown Philadelphia. The psychedelic sixties were a'borning, and dank light splayed about the room, a yellow mist that sponged out at the walls. WFIL–FM hummed folksy guitar music through loudspeakers in the rear. The circular table was covered with empty coffee cups, dead cigarette butts, and a thin coat of gray tobacco ash that blew into new patterns every time the front door opened.

"Who brought God into this, anyway?" Larry's gray eyes glistened as his jowls tightened. "Soul's the word, the inside muse that lets us see past the obvious. You know better than I do, Dimitri, how important the imagination is to artistic inspiration. Of all the arts, music relies most on it."

"It really comes down to a question of will," offered Bob Summers, a wiry hawk-nosed playwright. "We make our own inspiration by having the courage to take our destiny into our own hands. Depending on God, inspiration, or orgone energies begs the question."

"Which is?" I asked.

"Which is what?"

"What's the question we're begging?"

"Responsibility," Bob said. "Responsibility for our own fate, responsibility for power, for exercising our own will and shaping the world instead of being shaped by it."

"Hah! Immanuel Kant!" Dimitri shouted.

The front door opened and we abandoned the word game to watch three young women walk in. They all wore existentialist outfits matching my own—black sweaters and jeans. Though all four of us were married or had live-ins, all four of us undressed them with our eyes, more from male rivalry than real lust. The tallest of the trio, a fiery redhead, locked eyes with Dimitri and grinned as she sat at a side table. In a flash Dimitri stood and was on his way toward them. Bob sighed and looked toward the ceiling.

"Oh, how I need a good woman!" he moaned.

We laughed as he grimaced. Though calling one another friends, we secretly rejoiced at the ego hurts of our companions, hidden mockery that took the heat off our own lousy feelings. Some of the bitterness came from having to work at daytime jobs having little to do with our dream worlds.

In my case it meant writing a third novel while, from 8:30 to 5:00 every weekday, scheming up civil service exams for the city's personnel department. Juneau, who had moved in with me after arriving from Seattle, was a weekend sculptor and daytime reservations clerk for National Airlines. Dimitri, with a sonata and symphony performed at Tanglewood, supported a wife and an infant son teaching theory at the Curtis Institute of Music.

Bob lived off small monthly handouts donated by "patrons"—people on his supersecret "sucker list"— augmenting what his wife Dot earned from free-lance commercial artwork. Larry King, middle-aged actor who'd roomed with Henry Miller, was now directing little theater rehearsals for Bob's latest play. Fully supported by his longtime live-in Sylvia, he seemingly had least cause for bitterness: still he moaned and groaned with the worst of us. Most evenings after dinner we'd drop in at the coffee shop, with or without our women, joining a hodgepodge of actors, students, groupies, musicians, literary types, hipsters, and revolutionaries who drank overpriced cappuccino, flirted, and babbled incessantly.

We spent so little time at home mostly because when locked inside four walls, we had to confront our personal demons. My problem was chronic rage that destroyed any peaceful mood or setting. Even as a youngster I'd been brooding and morose, low man on a totem pole headed by a sullen father, overbearing mother, and much older, constantly feuding sister and brother. Now, even though crazy in love with Juneau, I lashed out at her at the smallest pretext.

Juneau and I rarely talked openly about our inner torments. Instead, we muzzled our festering truths and dreamed of great achievements, of one day becoming "beautiful people." Juneau had traded her own art-world ambitions for a share in mine, content to be the "great writer's wife" and not have to suffer directly the pain of having her own expressions criticized and rejected. We owned up to being a pair of psychic cripples trying to build a workable marriage. I was fond of saying, "Honey, we're both neurotic but at least our neuroses match." There was a big, dark hole inside us, though, that remained yearning and empty. Each of us demanded from the other what we did not have to give—peace and inner contentment. And we hated each other when we didn't get it. So we settled for a shared obsession to be "somebody special."

In our circle, "art" was god. Jack Kerouac, Pablo Picasso, Clifford Brown, and Albert Camus were its holy men, and Sigmund Freud its high priest. Anyone who didn't worship at the same shrine was unworthy of consideration. Anything that helped us chase a dream was "good"; whatever got in the way was "bad." And whenever our bubbles of illusion were pricked, which was almost every day, we medicated our egos with drugs.

One afternoon I came home from work, grumpy as usual, and slumped into the easy chair.

"Jimmy called," Juneau said.

"Jimmy who?" I asked.

"Jimmy Baldwin. He asked you to call as soon as you got home."

I flashed back to my student days in Paris five years earlier. James Baldwin had just published his first novel *Go Tell It on the Mountain,* to great reviews hailing him the new king of Afro-American writers. He appeared one evening at the Cafe Tournon across from the Assemblee Nationale, an American literary hangout where regulars included Richard Wright, William Gardner Smith, George Plimpton, and Truman Capote. As a Sorbonne student writing a first novel, I quickly discovered Baldwin was a confirmed homosexual on the make. But despite great all-night walks and literary talks along the Seine where we greeted the sun together, I maintained my heterosexual status—even after being warned that the literary world was thoroughly gay and I'd best go along to get along. I'd done neither, and though we traded a few letters afterward, I hadn't heard from him for two years.

Calling the number he'd left, I reached him at the Locust Theater. "What are you doing in Philly?" I asked.

"Apprenticing with Gadge Kazan, if you can believe it. We're in town for tryouts and of course I thought of you. Would you like to see the show? With your girlfriend, if that's who she is."

"Your play, Jimmy?"

"I only wish it were, baby. It's Tennessee Williams' *Sweet Bird of Youth,* with a marvelous cast—Paul Newman and Geraldine Page. How about coming to rehearsal this afternoon? And can you use two tickets for Wednesday?"

We talked a bit more and made arrangements to meet him at the theater. After I hung up, Juneau suggested throwing a party in Baldwin's honor at our place. It would be a way to repay old social debts and exalt ourselves with some reflected glory.

"We could invite Davis Grubb and make it a literary evening," I piped in.

Grubb, a hulking West Virginian, was a middle-aged ad copywriter who struck it rich with his novel *Night of the Hunter* that turned into a hit movie starring Robert Mitchum and Shelley Winters, hauntingly directed by Charles Laughton.

At rehearsal, Jimmy was tied up with Kazan and Williams, so we never got a chance to talk beyond a few brief greetings. Wednesday night we thoroughly enjoyed Newman, Page, and *Sweet Bird,* amazed at how all the rough spots had disappeared overnight. Then Baldwin, Juneau, and I went to a nearby restaurant to talk. Over ice cream and apple pie, I asked him to our place Friday night.

"I hate parties," he said, then grinned. "But for you, David—"

Jimmy's manner conveyed an intimacy that didn't seem warranted, but Juneau was impressed and I felt flattered. On our walk home, we began planning our guest list, and by Thursday night, after quickly nailing down Grubb who was thrilled at the chance to meet Baldwin, we had forty literary types lined up—mostly older professors and culture buffs panting at the prospect of partying with two famous writers. Juneau scoured the apartment and shampooed the carpets, and we stocked the tables with wine, snacks, and a huge pot of chili.

Though we'd specified 8:00 P.M., people started arriving at 7:15. Even Grubb showed up fifteen minutes early. Keeping the wine poured and the food plates replenished, Juneau and I stood back and watched would-bes and never-weres battle for the chance to corner Grubb and enjoy a few moments of celebrity glow until shouldered aside by someone else. As hosts, we felt smugly superior to the fawning and flattering small talk. Baldwin didn't show until about 8:30. The moment he walked through the door, the crowd surrounding Grubb melted away and engulfed the diminutive newcomer.

Grubb's reaction surprised us. We thought he'd be relieved to get some space. Instead he swallowed a pill, guzzled wine, and glowered enviously at the mob around his rival. Soon he could not contain himself and bellowed, "Baldwin! James Baldwin!"

An aisle opened as the crowd parted. Jimmy peered nearsightedly toward Grubb, who pushed through the opening and extended his hand to shake. But he leaned his body far back, out of intimacy range. Baldwin's eyes narrowed and sparked.

"You don't like black people, do you, Davis Grubb?" he asked.

"Why? How do you mean?" Grubb waved his hand, flustered.

"Am I wrong? Do you like blacks, then?"

"I'm from West Virginia," Grubb said. "We grew up with black people, so you've no call asking me that."

"You never did answer me, did you? You don't like black people. You don't feel comfortable around us. Now, why don't you just admit it!"

It was a remarkable exchange for two people who'd just met, and the guests, who had been raucously talking and laughing, in an instant grew deathly still. Tension built as Baldwin stared at Grubb, eyes bugging out, until Grubb lowered his head.

"I do feel guilty around Negroes," he said.

"Yes! And your guilt is precisely what feeds my rage!" Baldwin shouted.

"I can't help what my grandparents did," Grubb said. "I never had any slaves, —— it!"

"Then why do you feel guilt?"

"I dunno. I just do."

"I'll tell you why you do—because you never did condemn your folks for treating my folks worse than plow mules. Condemn them now, Grubb! Now's your chance to make good."

Davis hung his head but said nothing.

"Come on, denounce them! Say they did an evil thing and you're sorry. Go on, say it!"

Grubb kept silent.

"You disgust me," Baldwin said and started for the door.

When I got to his side and began apologizing for the confrontation, Jimmy winked and patted my shoulder. "Don't be silly, it's been fun," he confided. "I had to go anyhow, and the —— deserved it. Keep in touch, baby."

With Baldwin gone, the place cleared in ten minutes.

Grubb left last, staggering drunk and consoled by a local poet who helped him out the door. Still marveling over the evening, Juneau and I started cleaning up the debris. Some swine had crushed his cigarette butts into the carpet; another had dropped a sandwich on the floor, smearing mustard all over the place. But it was worth it. We'd stunned the local yokels, balanced our social ledger, and got to see David Grubb upstaged by a real expert.

♦

The art world, I'd found, was made up of two kinds of people—those who do and those who just talk about it. I was known as a doer. Four years before, my first novel, set in a Buck's County kid's camp, gained me a top New York agent at age twenty-three and earned some publisher encouragement, but no takers. Eighteen months later I finished a Dostoyevskian murder story set on the Penn State campus, drawing more admiration but no contract. With the wind temporarily out of my creative sails, I did what would become a life pattern—run for foreign soil. Taking off for Mexico, I started a third book, *The Century God Slept,* a semiautobiographical novel drawn on the coffee-shop characters I'd left back in Philadelphia.

In Mexico I first started smoking marjuana heavily, beginning after lunch and "poking up" every three hours until falling asleep. My only sober time down there was the four after-breakfast hours when I'd do my writing. Halfway through the *Century* draft, one afternoon at the beach I'd seen—and could not take my eyes off—a golden blonde vision in a two-piece swimsuit. Her name, I soon learned from the beachboys, was Juneau Alsin from Seattle, then modeling and acting in Mexican movies.

After admiring her from afar, I finally introduced myself. We talked, her sweet disposition melted my heart, and I was in love. As I probed her background, she confessed that acting was not her real calling. She'd studied at the San Francisco School of Fine Arts and found her true soul satisfaction in sculpting. The art connection did it for me. The next day I proposed marriage and spent a month courting her until my money ran out. I left for the States only after getting Juneau's promise to join me in Philadelphia. But while I'd been researching her, she'd been evaluating me . . . .

Before Mexico, I had done my share of traveling, worked in a variety of glamor jobs, and experienced different life styles. When I met David, I had been looking for answers to life's questions. Why was I born? What is life truly about? How could I find lasting happiness? Does God exist? Is there a meaning to the universe?

David had a vision of his own life, an all-consuming goal that gave it meaning. He was Jewish, so he would know about God, and I believed writers could see beyond the perplexities I was wrestling with. David seemed peaceful and kind, in charge of his life, whereas I felt engulfed by a sea of choices. When I got to Philadelphia, I asked David about God and His nature. Did he, in fact, believe in God?

"Yes," he answered. "There is order in the universe, and I'm convinced there is a Creator who made it so."

But he didn't know about a personal God. He felt we had to make our own ways in this world, that we were in charge of our own destinies. He was himself still trying to understand about God. I accepted David's understanding as the correct one. We could seek more answers together.

Soon after Juneau moved into my battered bachelor pad, she made it shine. Now, six months later, here we were down on our knees together cleaning up the aftermath of the Baldwin-Grubb face-off.

A few weeks after throwing the party, I finished *The Century God Slept.* Following the first flush of triumph over seeing it completed, I sent it to my agent. Convinced it was the most revolutionary work of art ever produced by a post-beatnik writer, Toni Strassman began sending it off to the list of prestigious publishers who had asked to see "Chagall's next work." The long wait began anew.

Over the past few years, the harsh realities of big-time publishing began to take their toll on my natural optimism. From the euphoric can't-miss certainty I felt after finishing my first manuscript, as each successive publisher took half a year to say no, I experienced withering expectations of money and fame along with a heart hardened by protective cynicism. Though I was getting tougher, I was paying a huge creative price.

The world seemed to be one huge conspiracy to keep me from writing, to steal my time, drain my energies, and kill my determination to hone my skills. Determined not to let the publishers grind me down, Juneau and I began saving our money for Europe. That meant no new clothes, no new LPs, no movies, restaurants, or expensive groceries. Every dollar we could squeeze from our take-home checks went into our getaway fund, and just knowing it was there helped our morale.

Our life together pointed to the same goal—my success as a writer. Juneau focused her own future and desires on my needs, but a steady stream of old girlfriends calling the apartment made her question my fidelity. Were we committed to each other, for better or for worse, or just carrying on a casual romance? That night, at the dinner table, we held hands and made our marriage vows to each other, pledging our love, lives, and loyalties until death parted us. We counted that day as our true wedding date. A later ceremony seemed redundant, for we were already joined in spirit.

The period between books, when I had to wait for my creative well to fill again, was a truly painful stretch. There was the agony of not doing what I was meant to do, magnified by a nagging fear that the well had run dry for the last time. This time, though, I was prepared. On the way back from Mexico, I'd smuggled a huge sweater bag full of top-grade marijuana across the border. Each day after work I'd roll a few joints, then Juneau and I would get stoned.

Grass was our sacrament. What prayer is to a believer, marijuana was for us. It tuned us into our inner selves, freeing our minds from worry, frustration, and doubt for the few hours the effect lasted. It slowed the rapid flow of ordinary thoughts, so I was able to apply the grass high for self-analysis, using notebooks and Freudian theory to hash over childhood hurts and hang-ups. Though I didn't believe in the Man who first said it, I believed what He taught: "You shall know the truth, and the truth shall make you free."

A common side effect of using cannabis was an attraction to occult subjects. Anything mystical, psychic, "spiritual," or way out beckoned like long-lost friends. One sleepless summer night, we discovered "The Long John Show," an all-night talk fest from WOR radio in New York. Hosted by ex-carnival barker John Nebel, in-studio guests ranged from a ridiculous "mystic barber" from Brooklyn who wore a copper antenna on his head and claimed to be in touch with star people to serious occult researchers like Jess Stearns, author of books on the famous trance medium Edgar Cayce.

One week the program focused on soul flight, the ability of the human spirit to leave the body and visit cities, countries, and even planets light years away. One guy kept referring to a "silver cord" stretching to incredible distances while still linked to the human body, warning that if that cord snapped, the spirit traveler died. Though soul travel appealed to our sense of the bizarre, it seemed like so much science-fiction bunk. As skeptics rooted firmly in Freudian evolutionary truth, we regarded "immortal souls and spirits" as the fanciful inventions of fearful folks unwilling to accept the finality of human death. But there was news waiting for me . . .

It was midweek. We'd just enjoyed a quiet evening reading and listening to Vivaldi, Bach, and Mozart LPs. Basking in a mellow baroque mood, we went to bed about eleven o'clock and fell quickly asleep. When I first came conscious again, I hadn't the slightest idea whether it was ten minutes or two hours later. It seemed just a snap of the fingers between the instant my eyes closed and blackness swirled in, to my awaking in the most unusual situation I'd ever encountered. There I was, drifting near the ceiling of our bedroom and looking down at a pair of bodies on the bed.

As a writer, I'm trained to notice details, stray bits of setting and atmosphere that help recreate reality on paper. As I hovered above the bed, I recall telling myself: "This is a very interesting development. Take good, clear mental notes to report on later." My attitude was one of relaxed curiosity, as though floating about disembodied were the most ordinary thing in the world to be doing on a Wednesday night in June.

I distinctly heard the ticking alarm clock, its hands showing 12:10, and the muffled sounds of night traffic drifting in from nearby streets. Gazing down to where my legs should have been, I saw only wispy cloudlike strands. Then a mist slowly emerged from Juneau's body, connected to her chest by a similar band of wispy white stuff. Though the fog that rose to join me had a rough human shape, its substance was amorphous like billowing smoke or white vapor. At the top-center of her projection, there was the rough outline of a face with cheeks, eyes, and a grinning mouth. Suddenly, her arms, like grasping pseudopods, reached out to grasp me. An intuitive flash warned me the embrace might be fatal. The instant I thought it, I found myself wriggling back into my chest. I sat up in bed, fully inside my body.

My heart pounded fearfully as I tried to make sense of it all. Oddly enough, between the time of floating and re-entering the flesh, I never lost consciousness. One moment I was made of wafting smoke, the next I was encased in solid flesh. Looking over at Juneau, I found her fast asleep, breathing deeply. I checked out the room and assured myself nothing had changed. The clock now read 12:16. My heartbeat had slowed, and beyond a lingering irritation over Juneau's grabbing for me, I was none the worse for wear.

But my outlook had changed. No longer could I accept the belief that man was just an evolved animal, a flesh-bound robot whose chemicals dissolved with death. Now, beyond a shadow of a doubt, I knew there was a part of me that was immaterial, a part that contained my consciousness and identity—a part that could leave my body and still be alive. I had to accept the truth of the human soul.

How could I be so sure this hadn't been just a vivid night dream? The same way you are sure you are really reading a book called *The Sunshine Road* and not merely dreaming you're reading it. There is an unmistakable difference between sleeping fantasy and wakeful reality—awake is awake and I, just as you, know that difference. Resting on that truth, I fell quickly into a sound, undisturbed sleep. I was never again to be aware of leaving my body, though a few nights later Juneau woke me.

"Stop that!" she yelled.

"Stop what?" I mumbled.

"Oh," she said. "There you are on the bed. I thought I heard you calling me from up there." She pointed to the ceiling.

"I know," I replied, and went back to sleep.

The following week a new book shaped itself in my mind. The urge to write was joined with an equally powerful compulsion to do it all under the spell of a marijuana high, using automatic writing techniques described by trance mediums. All my previous books had been crafted stone sober, without drugs or drink to inspire them. Obeying this inner call, I started all-night sessions at the typewriter, scarcely aware of what I was doing. Inside six lost weeks that seemed more like days, I completed a fictionalized journal I initially called *An Experience,* for want of a better title.

It told the story of a young college student who yearned to regain his childhood connection to honesty and inner truth. Packing camping gear into a duffel bag, he took off during his summer break for the Maine woods where he aimed to "get it all together" while pretending to be a deaf mute to avoid having to socialize. To his horror, he found the evil and hypocrisy he hated in the outside world really inhabited his own mind, soul, and nervous system. Along with this understanding he uncovered some of nature's secrets, rediscovered God as Spirit, rejoiced, suffered, and died.

Since I usually took a year or more per book, this forty-day wonder was something of a miracle. Reading it through in the cold, sober light of day, I was amazed at how clear, powerful, and classical the writing was, very unlike my usual style. It was as though it had been written by someone else. To acknowledge that other-world legacy, I typed out a dedication page reading "Remembering Rupert Brooke," crediting an English poet who died in 1915 of blood poisoning—precisely as did the hero of my newest work.

Juneau read the novella at one sitting, marveling over its gripping power and depth. So off it went to Toni with a short note, and I rested from my labors. Again drained of creative juice, I filled the gap with coffee-shop bouts, partying and daydreaming about the fame, wealth, and freedom from jobs that would soon be ours.

As habitual night people, Juneau and I stayed up most workdays to 1:00 or 2:00 A.M. and on weekends closer to sunrise. One wee-hour hangout was a radio talk-show broadcast from a Walnut Street restaurant, hosted by a transplanted New Yorker named Steve Allison. On my return from Paris I'd guested with Allison several times, billed as a "rising young literary lion." I enjoyed being treated as a celebrity and having the maitre d' seat us at front-row tables whenever we dropped by.

One night he had a retired air force major at the mike, "blowing the cover" on the government's conspiracy to hide its flying saucer investigations. As a former intelligence officer, Major Donald Keyhoe made a convincing case for mysterious visitations from advanced space people, so much so the next night we found ourselves attending his talk at the Theosophical Society's headquarters on Chestnut Street.

About forty people were crammed into the small two-room suite, mostly housewives, widow-aged women, and middle-aged men wearing cheap suits and sports coats. Keyhoe, a balding unimpressive man in his fifties, rattled off a bunch of reportedly suppressed air force encounters with extraterrestrial aircrafts. He showed intriguing slides of saucer photos that he linked to a New Age philosophy of unisex spirituality he said the space people wished to introduce to our bedeviled planet. It was the next step, he confided, "in an evolution of consciousness that will usher in the era of peace on earth and good will toward men." Chatting with him afterward, we were intrigued by the way he tied in Darwinian evolution to a peace-love philosophy that warmed out godless hearts. He cited actual contacts he had investigated, and assured us these interplanetary visitors were advanced, truly godlike beings.

We started reading everything we could find on saucers,

space people, and Aquarian Age philosophy. One day while rooting through the local library's ESP shelves, we came across the "Betty books" by Stuart Edward White. A prolific author of Western novels and nature writing, White compiled a series of books the author's wife had dictated while in a trance, speaking aloud the words of controlling spirits while her husband recorded their utterances.

Betty's "spirit guides"—who called themselves "Invisibles"—dismissed notions of heaven and hell as mere ignorant superstition. After we die, they explained, we merely join a society of Invisibles and influence life on earth according to our former loving or wicked predilections. They stressed that life's problems are really opportunities in disguise. The harder we strive to solve them, the greater our spiritual growth and the better off we will be in our next phase of existence. "Resistance overcome is the key to progress," they preached. Eventually, higher souls evolve to new, more rarified "kingdoms of heaven" with infinite levels of growth still ahead.

According to this adapted Buddhist doctrine, evolved souls may choose to hang around earth and serve as spirit guides to loving human "sensitives" who use trances to bring "spiritual truth" to their fellows. These are called "mediums" or "trance channelers." Out of compassion for the pitiful wretches trapped in ignorance, every few centuries an exalted Invisible may choose to be reborn as a "Master." Jesus Christ is named as one such incarnated Master, as is Buddha, Plato, Confucius, Moses, and Mohammed.

Although we were open to the many philosophies we were exposed to, we did resist this theory, as Juneau remembers.

But we balked at the idea of reincarnation. When our friends tried to sell us on it, David argued, "Even granting it might be true, we can't base our lives on such a theory. It would make life meaningless. Why try to accomplish anything now when you can wait and do it in a next lifetime?"

Reincarnation goes hand in hand with the

*notion of karma, which teaches that every soul
carries its spiritual growth from one lifetime to the
next. Bad things that happen to a person are payment for evil deeds in a past life, good things are
rewards earned last lifetime around. So we've no
need to feel sympathy for a suffering person. He and
she are getting just what they deserve. Good or bad,
all is fated by what you do.*

*When reincarnationists came on too strong,
David would tell them, "If it's such an exalted faith,
how come India is such a pathetic, poverty-cursed
hell hole? Millions starve over there, and nobody
around them even cares. Is that what you want here?
Just take a trip over to Calcutta, and see what Eastern gurus do to their own people!"*

*But the Invisibles' message of spiritual growth
through overcoming life's challenges was comforting.
Besides helping us feel good about ourselves, it made
our pains and struggles all seem worthwhile. And it
gave us hope of an afterlife in a lovely trouble-free
heaven, much like an idealized Acapulco on its best
day.*

As devotees of the making-it lifestyle, Juneau and I
found it easy to graft Betty's philosophy onto our life mix of
work, drugs, pleasure, and self-glorification. Our friends
found Betty's "truth" equally attractive as they reached for
their own brass rings on life's merry-go-round. Al DeLeo, for
one.

Al was an ex-professional boxer who at twenty-four
bought himself a tenor sax, enrolled at Granoff School of
Music, and earned his living waiting tables at an Italian restaurant while dreaming of a career as a jazz bopper. He was
married to Wendy, the fresh-faced daughter of a high-school
principal who had wished her a loftier fate. Al and I would
get high, listen to jazz giants on our hi-fi, and try to play
together at impromptu jam sessions, he on tenor, me on
trumpet. Unhappily, Al had no real musical talent.

So he found his truth in reincarnation theory and began

going to meetings at the Theosophical Society founded by nineteenth-century occultist Helena Blavatsky. Fervor for jazz began to fade as he spent most of his free time getting stoned on drugs and reading mystical books. One afternoon we dropped by his place to find Al, Wendy, and their new baby admiring his latest handiwork—he had strung violet beads all around their bedroom, lending it a Middle Eastern Casbah touch.

"It gets us closer to our higher centers," he explained, touching his heart. "It's where it's at, man."

Noting Wendy's bruised eye, masked by heavy layers of makeup, we knew he'd been beating her again. Wendy confided to Juneau that Al had found fault with the pasta she'd cooked for him; it was not Italian enough for his tastes. Evidently, those higher centers had yet to cure his mean streak.

Our local librarian, who was remarkably knowledgeable about occultism, touted us onto a book by Sir Arthur Conan Doyle. Best known for his Sherlock Holmes series, Doyle was cofounder of the London Society for Psychical Research, which published a series of books proving the survival of bodily death, thought transference, and other paranormal manifestations.

One test involved threading a needle through a cork, dangling it into a wine bottle and setting it on a solid surface. Since no air or wind currents can get inside to move the needle, the experimenter can move the needle simply by willing it—if "mental energy" truly exists. Soon we had a bottled needle standing on a sturdy wooden trunk, and seated cross-legged on the floor, Juneau and I took turns trying to move it telekinetically (tele=distance; kinesis=motion).

Then we discovered a paradox. The harder we tried, the more sure we could be that the needle wouldn't even wiggle. But the moment we relaxed, things really started to happen. The key to this power, we learned, was the gift of surrendering our will power and just "letting it happen." Both Juneau and I became adept at getting the needle to wiggle mightily, but not predictably. At any given moment, there was no way to tell whether it would move or not until it actually did so. The "power" was not really ours to command.

Tiring of needles, I turned to larger objects. After dinner one night I screwed a dull red bulb into a floor lamp anchored by a heavy brass base. Stretching prone on the living room sofa, I focused my attention on that lamp, and as I relaxed into a semitwilight state, I sensed I was connecting with it and visualized it moving. Soon the shade started to vibrate, then the entire lamp rocked so violently I feared it would crash down and break. I was so deep in concentration that when Juneau called "David!" from the kitchen, a sharp pain seared my chest and between my shoulder blades where connections to the lamp seemed to emanate. Alarmed over shattering my "silver cord" of ectoplasmic soul substance, I leaped up, ran into the kitchen, and berated poor Juneau over the danger of startling me when I was into that red-light trance.

We heard about the experiments Dr. J. B. Rhine was doing down at Duke University. I'd always been fascinated by the possibility of mental telepathy, so we experimented with some of Rhine's methods. I made up a set of flash cards by drawing simple symbols—a triangle, rectangle, circle, wavy line. One of us went into an adjoining room, while the other would try to tune in to the "sender" and mark down the sequence of symbols.

Other times we would place the cards face down, shuffle them around, and try to read them by touch (psychometry). Or we might try sending mental pictures across space. I would lie on the bed, trying to relax my mind and brain, while David was in another room concentrating on photos clipped from magazines. Though we didn't score any better than the law of averages, we were convinced that if we practised enough we could develop this ability. Stories abounded about people who communicated this way, saving a loved one's life by receiving mental images at times of danger. Such a talent would expand our powers, and give us a real advantage in life's competition. So we kept trying, but when we

could not improve our mediocre scores, we got
bored with our Rhine cards.

Next I tried levitation. My model was the British psychic D. D. Home who, in the presence of Arthur Conan Doyle and William Crookes, one warm spring night floated out the window of Doyle's London flat and floated back in an adjoining window. Both researchers had passed their hands under and over Home's body to be sure no invisible wires were involved, and so were able to verify the reality of Home's skills. I spent two full weeks of after-dinner efforts in our bedroom, bathed in dim red light, vainly trying to make my body lift weightlessly off the bed. But flying without wings proved beyond my modest powers. When once again Juneau almost scared me out of my body by calling my name, I gave up the levitation experiments. We had no idea we were playing around with dark and dangerous spiritual forces.

Meanwhile, Bob Summers—whose last produced play had closed after three performances—began to confide in me about his new Nietzschean life view. Friedrick Nietzsche, German philosopher and son of a Lutheran minister, formulated the idea of the "Superman." Preaching the superiority of a natural elite, he called for exalted beings who would use will power to rise above Christian concepts of good and evil, crush "decadent democracy," and so rule the masses who yearn for such bondage. Hitler and his Nazis borrowed much of their inspiration from Nietzsche.

Bob asked me to read his new play, *The Parasite*. I found it enchanting, full of ideas, rich with G. B. Shaw-like wit and humor. I was less enamored with its hero George, who vows never again to work for wages but instead lives by sponging off friends and associates. George struck me as a spoiled brat, full of his own superiority and unwarranted arrogance—and ultimately tiresome. As I shared my reactions with Bob, I sensed his anger, but he choked it back and merely praised my "insight." So we talked far into the night about the noblesse oblige of creative people, the nature of genius, and the accident of fate that had endowed us both with such exalted powers. The next day as I thought about our discussion, I sensed that Bob—like his mentor Nietzsche—was courting madness.

After dinner a few evenings later, the phone rang. It was Toni in New York, bubbling with excitement as she related how Burroughs Mitchell, famed Scribner's editor who launched James Jones, had just finished reading *An Experience* and wanted to see me in New York as soon as possible. How soon could I get there?

"Tomorrow?" I asked.

The next morning Toni and I were ushered into the editorial wing of the Scribner Building, a series of wood-paneled cubicles that had seen writers like John Dos Passos, Ernest Hemingway, and Thomas Wolfe tread across its aristocratic corridors. Even as we sat waiting on the wooden bench outside, James Jones bustled past carrying under his right arm a mass of manuscript that would be transformed into *Some Came Running*.

After fifteen minutes, the secretary came out and ushered us into the chief editor's chamber. A middle-aged man, slim, elegant, and bland-looking in his tweed suit, Mitchell invited us to sit. Then he just sat there twirling a pencil between his fingers for thirty seconds that seemed like minutes before he suddenly swiveled his chair in my direction.

"Your book . . . ," he said, indicating the boxed manuscript on his desk.

He left behind a silence so gaping I blurted out "Yes?" just to break the tension.

"This book," he said, "this *Experience* of yours . . ."

Another, even longer pause. This time I locked my tongue.

Mitchell grimaced, then said, "This book is not a novel."

It was like a bomb had gone off in my brain. "Not what? Not a novel?" I stammered.

Toni grinned at Mitchell like an idiot, sensing a dark turn.

"Exactly right," he said. "It hasn't the form of a novel. It's not really what I expected of you after that last one you did on the beatnik people. We had high hopes you would bring us something patterned more after that one, something more visceral in the sense of . . ."

He rambled on until he ran out of fuel.

"I'm really sorry it has to be this way. I'm afraid we're just not the right publisher for the sort of thing you're doing and the new directions you seem to be taking."

I tried to reply, but words couldn't squeeze past the clog in my throat. Battling a flood of emotion, I lost and started to cry. Walking through the corridors out to the street, I choked back sobs. Toni mumbled a few consolatory sentences, but I never heard what she said. Shaking my head numbly, I turned toward Forty-second Street and the Port Authority bus terminal, navigating through a fog of sorrow. By the time I got back to Philadelphia, grief had turned to angry despair. I hated Burroughs Mitchell and all smug New Yorkers, envious talent killers who had sold out their own ideals for security and now got their kicks trying to murder a young writer's dream.

Juneau and I talked late into the night. I told her if I didn't get away from here, New York, the whole blinking country, the little spark that made me a writer and an artist was in danger of being snuffed out. In a shared spirit of adventure, Juneau agreed. It was time to cash in our chips, pull up stakes, and challenge our destiny.

3

Off to Europe

e closed out our bank accounts, and Juneau used her employee discount from National Airlines to buy cut-rate air fares to Brussels. Just before we left for the airport, she had second thoughts. Suppose I forgot my vows, got mad and took off, leaving her penniless and helpless over there? Assuring her of my undying loyalty, I literally had to pry her fingers off the radiator before I could get her into the taxi.

Helicoptering into Paris with bellies fighting the heaves, we stopped off for a week's stay. Though it had been five years since I'd last been to the City of Lights as a wide-eyed student, nothing had changed, including the open contempt Parisians enjoyed spewing on visiting Americans.

While introducing Juneau to my old Left Bank haunts, we ran into an old friend at the Cafe Tournon, the black novelist William Gardner Smith. Over cafe au lait we heartily trashed the latest crop of fair-haired American writers, but I couldn't help noticing the deeply etched circles under Bill's eyes that hadn't been there before. When I asked about his latest work-in-progress, his evasive double talk told of creative troubles along with the physical—a burnout at thirty-nine.

The day before we were to leave France, I followed an

impulse and dropped in to see Albert Camus. This was just before he was awarded the Nobel Prize, and though greatly admired as a writer, he'd not yet assumed the demigod status he would be accorded just before his death and, of course, ever since.

Camus was a rarity among famous writers—he was available to other, younger writers. Continually suffering entreaties from impatient, desperate apprentices like myself, he nonetheless treated us all with dignity and respect. In this instance, he even offered to read my work and offer advice. Leaving him a copy of *An Experience,* we took the train to Italy and spent a week on the Italian Riviera. After losing my raincoat, being besieged by hustlers on every street and square, and having to pay $5.25 for a tiny plate of spaghetti without sauce, we opted to head for Spain where the living was easier and cheaper.

Sailing out of Barcelona, we settled into a seaside Majorcan villa surrounded by scenic island marvels where I started another "search" book. As soon as I realized it was just a disguised replay of *An Experience,* I junked it and launched another novel, driven by the desperate realization that our money was running out.

The next few months flew by. The isolation made me more insecure than ever, and jealousy became a real problem. Every time we'd walk down the street or stop into a cafe, I watched Juneau's eyes to see if she was glancing at any of the men checking her out. No sooner did her eyes raise off the sidewalk than I felt sure she was flirting and committing spiritual adultery. Volcanic rage lurked just beneath the surface, ever ready to explode. That neurotic, unmerited jealousy kept our life hellish during a time of relative calm.

Lovely Majorca, for us, proved to be nothing more than an idyllic Devil's Island of the soul. Finally, there was just enough money left to pay our fares back home, so late that summer we shipped out on the Israeli liner *Zion* from Barcelona.

———————————◆———————————

Back in Philadelphia, Juneau got her airlines job back, and I landed a job as epidemiological investigator with the city's Health Department. This high-sounding title demanded I call on bars, brothels, and rundown apartment houses to locate and persuade folks exposed to social diseases to come in for a blood test or—in cases where that was impractical—to draw a blood sample from a vein right then and there. At nightfall my lifestyle turned literary, but gonorrhea, syphilis, and TB filled my days.

Late one afternoon when I was haunting a black bar in south Philly, a tawny prostitute with bleached red hair tipped me off about a suspected syphilis carrier on my contact list. Climbing rickety wooden stairs to the third floor of a rundown converted townhouse, I found his room and knocked loudly on the door.

A man's voice growled "Yeah?"

Identifying myself as a city agent, I turned the doorknob and walked in. Mr. Carter, a barrel-chested man in his midfifties, sat on a stuffed chair facing me.

"That's far enough," he said. "Whattya want?"

Explaining he'd been exposed to a contagious disease and needed a blood test, I opened my case.

"This won't take but a few seconds," I said.

As I brought the rubber tie and needle out of my case, Mr. Carter reached down beside his chair and came up with a metallic blue pistol pointing at my jaw.

"You ain't gonna do nothin'," he said.

"It doesn't really hurt," I replied, my heart thumping against my ribs.

"Listen you ——," he said. "You get outta here or I'll blow your —— head off!"

His pistol extended menacingly as he repeated the threat. Suddenly I took off, racing down the stairs, three at a time. Reaching the relative safety of the streets, I waited ten minutes for my rubbery legs to stiffen up, took out my report book, and checked the "refused test" box opposite Harold Carter's name. It could have been worse.

The newspapers were reporting a flurry of UFO sightings. Pilots were spotting them all over the city, day and night.

One day after lunch, I was returning to the

*National Airlines ticket office when I was stopped by
a mob of people overflowing the sidewalks clear out
to the street. Close by, I overheard some well-dressed
businessmen talking about the Air Force jets that had
just roared past chasing a UFO, only to lose contact
because of its unbelievable speed.*

*Convinced these were interplanetary visitors,
we yearned to see a UFO ourselves. Or, better yet,
actually get a look at one of the aliens. We arranged
several "saucer parties" on our rooftop, inviting
friends whose interest was as serious as our own.
We'd all gaze into the sky for hours, watching for
strange lights moving in the heavens. We were sure
that these highly evolved, superior beings would be
able to discern that we were friendly earthlings, and
give us some sign they knew we were there.*

*As believers in evolution, since their civilizations
were unquestionably much older than ours, we were
sure they had evolved much farther. Could they not
teach us secrets from their own greater intellects?
Certainly one of these truths would be that earth
must unite our many nations into one world,
operating under one government, expanding our
horizons to prepare for membership in the interplanetary universe.*

One evening just before dinner, the phone rang and I
answered. It was my mother, and her voice was choked with
emotion.

"Son," she said. "It's . . . it's your father."

"What about him, Ma?"

"He's . . . oy, he's not good. What can I say? Please
come over right away!"

My mom did not tend to hysteria, so I hopped on a
subway train and headed the six miles north to Logan where
my folks lived. While we were in Majorca, my father had
been fired from his job of thirty-two years as a wholesale
grocery salesman. Typically, it was a case of the younger generation taking over a family business from their father and

cleaning out "dead wood"—in this case, a man who had helped build Steinhart & Co. from a struggling garage operation into a multimillion dollar complex. I thought of Arthur Miller's Willy Loman and the uncanny parallel to his *Death of a Salesman* story.

When I got to the house, my mom whispered, "He's all right now."

"What do you mean, he's all right?" I asked. "What's he been doing?"

"Don't ask," she answered.

Inside the living room, my father sat on the sofa, his head in his hands. My sister and brother-in-law were in the kitchen, whispering.

"Hi, Dad," I called. "How you doin'?"

He didn't reply.

"I missed you. Got any poems for me?"

Early in life he worked as a reporter for the Jewish *Forward,* a Yiddish language newspaper, but slave wages prompted him to give up journalism for sales. Still, the muse drove him to write narratives in rhyming English and Yiddish prose, and I got a kick out of the humor and bite in his words. Only now he did not respond at all, frozen in his black mood.

"C'mere, I want you to see something." My mother led me down the basement stairs and pointed to the water pipes wired to the ceiling beams. A clothesline dangled down, frayed at the end where it had snapped under a great weight.

"Oh, no!" I groaned. "When did this happen?"

"He's been bad like this the last few weeks," she said, sobbing briefly. "First he wanted me to turn on the gas oven, sit with him in the kitchen, close the doors and 'go to sleep' together. Then he told me he saw a hand coming out of the wall, trying to grab him, and voices talk to him. Another night he tried to choke me, and today I find this rope . . . I don't know what to do, Son!"

"I'll talk to him, Mom."

With foreboding in my heart, I put on my most cheerful face and went back to the living room. Sitting beside my father, I put my arm around his shoulder.

"What's the matter, Dad?" I asked. "I hear you've been having a tough time. Feel like talking about it?"

No answer, not even a shrug.

"I remember when I was a kid and you used to take me with you Saturdays to call on customers. Remember, Dad? You used to let me carry your sample satchel, and I felt so proud!"

Morbid brooding silence. His despair started getting to me. "Dad, please!" I cried. "You can't just give up! You got to fight back!" No answer. In desperation, I turned to the Source of help I wasn't sure existed. "Dad, let's get down on our knees and pray to God. Only He can help us now!"

For the first time since I walked in, he took his hands away from his face and looked at me incredulously. "Are you crazy?" he asked. Covering his face again, he retreated back into his cocoon of despair.

I went to the kitchen and joined the others. "What did the doctor say?" I asked.

"He doesn't want to see the doctor," my sister Bert said.

"What's that got to do with it? The man's sick. He's trying to kill himself!"

"Maybe it will pass," my mother said.

"And maybe he'll strangle you or turn on the gas," I said. "I'm calling the hospital."

A mild argument ensued as the others considered how much it would "shame" Harry, how much a hospital cost, how he would never forgive them if they turned him in. I settled the matter by calling nearby Pennsylvania Psychiatric Hospital. Within thirty minutes an ambulance arrived, and as they put him into a straightjacket and led him out, tears flowed like bitter wine.

They wouldn't let us visit the first week while they treated him with electrodes and drugs. The next time I saw him was in the hospital cafeteria, and he was wearing pajamas and a robe. The change was remarkable. Though his eyes were still dull, they had lost the haunted look, and he responded to questions, even asking how my writing was going. Three weeks later he was dressed in slacks and a sport shirt. His blue eyes had regained their warm glow, and he showed me a poem he had written, taking off on some of the attendants and other patients. According to his doctor, the acute schizophrenic episode was slowly on the mend. Though he would need drugs to control the depression, there was a good chance he would be released in a few months.

My dad was discharged from the hospital in early October. It seemed a new anti-depressant drug was working a miracle in his life. Upbeat, optimistic, and full of fight, he was now making a comeback at age fifty-six. Arranging wholesale buying privileges with grocery suppliers, he'd loaded a station wagon with samples and begun calling on all his old mom-and-pop store customers. Without the giant overhead of Steinhart & Co., he was able to offer pickles, olives, and other specialties at far lower prices, so they were happy to give him their business along with their blessings.

More than that, he began reaching out to know me better. All my life growing up, I had known him as a stiff, grumpy overseer. He had never put his arm around me or hugged me. Instead, his usual greeting involved grinding a knuckle into the top of my head until I cried out. Just before dinner one night, our doorbell rang, and Juneau buzzed back to release the street door. When we opened the door to our hallway, my father stood there, satchel under his arm and a smile on his face. It was the first time anyone from my family had visited since Juneau and I were married.

"Dad!" I said. "Come on in!"

I hugged him, and this time he hugged back, bringing tears to my eyes. We exchanged small talk, he gave us cans of stuffed olives and artichokes, then broached the real purpose of his visit.

"Don't you think you should be closer to your mother?" he asked. "You don't know how much it hurts her when you don't come over. Maybe you and Juneau can come for dinner Friday night."

"We'd love to, wouldn't we, honey?"

"You bet we would," Juneau said. "What time do you want us there?"

"The sooner the better. It's the Sabbath meal, a very special meal in a Jewish family."

"Hey, that's great, Dad. Did we ever tell you how much we love you?"

He beamed happily as Juneau hugged him, followed by me. I'd never felt closer or been prouder of him.

"Have you been under a sunlamp, Mr. Chagall?" Juneau asked.

It was only then I noticed his tanned cheeks.

"No, not really," he said. "Well, I have to go."

We saw him out and I began raving over his new outlook. "He's like a new man," I said. "I hardly recognize him as my father."

"I don't like the way he looks," Juneau said. "Did you see the yellow in his eyes?"

"No," I replied.

"He's got a bad case of jaundice," she said. "I know the look from when I had hepatitis. You'd better call Chaika and have her get him to the doctor."

I phoned my mother, who admitted noticing the tanning for the past week.

"I'll take him to the doctor first thing tomorrow," she said.

"You promise?"

"I promise, I promise! What's the matter with you?"

After work the following day, I tried calling my family but no one answered. In the middle of dinner the phone rang. It was Mom, calling from the hospital.

"Your father is very sick," she said.

It took us fifteen minutes to get to Hahnemann Hospital, where we were allowed to visit just a few moments. It was a horrifying scene. Tubes protruded from his arms and nose while he lay there helplessly, groaning and shaking his head. It was hard to believe he was the same man we'd seen the day before. Out in the corridor, the doctor gave us a grim prognosis.

"He's got acute toxic hepatitis," he said, lips frozen in a straight line like a mannequin in a men's store. "It's an extremely severe case. The next seventy-two hours are crucial."

"What are his chances?" I asked.

He shook his head but said nothing.

"Fifty-fifty?"

"There's very little of his liver left," he said. "The liver is one of the few body organs that has the capacity to regenerate itself, but in his case . . ."

That night in bed I closed my eyes but did very little sleeping. For the first time in a long time, I prayed to a God I really didn't believe in, fervently vowing that if He healed my dad, I would know He was who He said He was and worship Him. I never realized until that moment how much I loved the old man, who really wasn't all that old.

The next day I phoned the hospital several times, only to learn he was still critical. That night when we went to see him, he was in a coma. Four days later he was dead. At his graveside, a light rain fell. They gave me a little yarmulke to wear while his rabbi praised him as a good Jew who served his synagogue, his God, and his family with good humor and dedication. As his only living son, I had the honor of throwing the first shovelful of dirt on his coffin.

Little good God and his synagogue had done him. While my mom, my sister, and Juneau sobbed, I brooded over the bitter irony that just when Harry Chagall seemed to be getting his life together, it was taken from him. And he never got the chance to gloat over his son, the published writer. The next month I turned twenty-eight, but we held no celebration to mark the event.

♦

Just before Christmas, the postman brought a note from Toni Strassman. Inside the envelope she'd enclosed a letter Albert Camus had written me in care of her office, the only address stamped on the manuscript I'd given him. It was a wonderful letter, supportive, and encouraging to a fault. Among his comments were the following words, "While reading *An Experience,* I was reminded of Thoreau's *Walden.* I was moved by the feeling of nature and truth that one finds on every one of these pages. You may use my name in any way it may be helpful, and you have my best wishes for all that you may do."

His words launched us into outer space. Dashing off photocopies of Camus's letter, I sent it to a dozen major New York firms claiming to publish "literature." Only one—Knopf—asked to read the book and smartly rejected it because they "didn't see a sufficient market for the work to justify taking it on."

This time I was not nearly so demolished. By now I'd come to expect such slavish devotion to profits by those New York guardians of popular culture. Meanwhile our savings continued to mount and, late that winter when the Swedish Academy awarded the Nobel Prize in Literature to Albert Camus, we determined to follow our dreams to Scandinavia.

Packing hi-fi, books and clothes, we left our dog with Patti and Ronny Weingrad, two close friends with hearts bigger than their heads. Ronny was an advertising man who had roomed with me in Mexico, Patti was an actress doing voiceovers for commercials, and Juneau and I served as witnesses at their wedding. Giving them charge of Sarah, our beloved mongrel, was symbolic of the real trust between us.

They saw us off at 30th Street Station as we boarded the train to Montreal, from where we sailed on the Greek liner *Arkadia* to Bremerhaven. Arriving in Stockholm, we found the city's colorful shops, narrow cobbled streets and tasty mix of the old and modern, nothing short of enchanting. The Swedes themselves—reserved, courteous, yet fierce defenders of their privacy—have managed to stay free and democratic and not fight a war for over two hundred years. Though they are overtaxed, poverty is practically extinct, and they have a highly advanced social conscience.

From the first day we arrived, Sweden embraced us as adopted children. While Raoul Wallenberg's sister Nina (from the famed banking family) summered abroad, we rented her beautifully furnished home on the suburban island of Lidingo.

Within a week we'd made friends among some of the nation's top writers. One best-selling novelist, Jascha Golowanjuk, threw a party in our honor where we "skoaled" one another with aquavit, traded ideas, and worshiped at the altar of literature. Armed with copies of my novella—which I'd retitled *Diary of a Deaf Mute*—I called on three of the nation's leading publishers and left them reading copies of the manuscript.

While waiting, we filled our days attending concerts and plays, walking the streets of Stockholm and joining nightly bull sessions with writers and other culture buffs where we learned to appreciate the high regard Swedes have for Americans. One morning our *postbud*—mail carrier—delivered a letter postmarked Philadelphia. Inside was a cryptic note from Bob Summers, "playfully" disguised as a "Top Secret, Eyes Only" dispatch.

As we read past the "intelligence agency" format, it seemed Bob planned to join us soon for his own "Scandinavian campaign." Sure enough, a few weeks later he called from a small hotel in downtown Stockholm, and we invited him to stay with us. Settling him into our attic apartment, we celebrated our reunion that night with a blast of wine and grass, then filled each other in on developments.

After smuggling new luggage into his apartment, Bob had secretly packed his belongings and left a letter for his wife, Dot, on the kitchen table. In it he explained his need to go overseas and spend a year trying to get his plays produced. Since the state would define it as desertion, she could apply for welfare and get regular checks for her dependent children.

The very next day, Bob lost no time embarking on his Scandinavian campaign. Calling on Steve Hopkins, an old naval intelligence buddy working as a writer for the English-language edition of the Swedish business magazine *Industria,* he milked him for contacts. We introduced him to some of our new friends, and soon he had worked up a list of the top theatrical producers, including names to throw at them for reference. Working the phone furiously, he set up meetings where he pitched the revolutionary nature of his plays, the impossible situation on Broadway, and why Sweden was the natural launching place for New Wave dramatists like himself—leaving behind a reading copy of *The Parasite* to prove his point.

It soon grew clear that Bob felt himself in a feverish

competition to "achieve success" before I did. In a nonstop barrage, he stressed how he would use his prestige and contacts to help me find a publisher—the moment he signed his own production contract, of course.

"It all comes down to finances," he explained. "There's infinitely more money in the theater than in book publishing. That's why playwrights are so rich and novelists so poor. My good friend Sydney Omarr had his heart broken when his novel, *My Bed Has Echoes,* earned him just $630. Can you believe it! Now Omarr's hacking out a crummy astrology column for newspapers, his zeal totally crushed. Poor Sydney—but don't you worry, David, I'll take care of you once I'm set up."

As it turned out, Bob would not get the chance to prove his generosity. Ten days later I got a call from Ake Lofgren, head editor for the leading Social Democrat party publisher Raben and Sjogren. "Your book is just extraordinary," he said. "We wish to bring it out next spring!" When we met in his office to discuss contract and translator, he looked me hard in the eye and asked, "Did you really write this book?" It was the most profound if backhanded compliment I'd ever received, and I beamed as I assured him I was its author. Of course I told him nothing about the automatic writing or my invisible helpers.

When the contract arrived in the mail, I compared it to a sample U.S. contract from the Authors Guild and found the Swedish one superior in virtually every clause. Signing smartly, we took it to the post office and celebrated with a fabulous smorgasbord feast at a nearby restaurant. While we were ordering our beverages, Bob couldn't take his eyes off a young blonde girl sitting two tables away. In an attempt to impress her, he leaned across the table with a forced grin curling his lips.

"Now we're sitting here having a good time," he said. "We're ordering our food, enjoying the sights as Americans in Stockholm, full of life and joy, ready for adventure." His tone was flat, as though quoting directions from a play, and Juneau and I laughed at his setting his own stage for the girl across the way.

At home later that afternoon, we could hear him up in the attic muttering, cursing, and shouting. "The fools! They'll pay. Every last one of them! In due course, my friends, we'll see the wheels of destiny churn, and then the truth will out. The idiots. —— their wretched pea brains!"

Just before dinner, we were in the atrium drinking coffee when his skin suddenly turned metallic gray like a submarine. I had never seen anything like it before, and it frightened me.

"Are you all right, Bob?" I asked. He was so enrapt he never even heard me.

"Bob!" I grabbed him, fearing a stroke or heart attack. "You okay, Bob?"

Rousing himself, he stammered, "Sure . . . of course. What makes you think anything's wrong?"

His voice was so queer and unlike him, I thought he might be possessed by an evil spirit. Later I mentioned my fear to Juneau, who dismissed the idea. She'd witnessed Bob's catatonic spell but ascribed it to his scheming jealousy. In any case, he never repeated that performance, so we dismissed it as an unexplained oddity.

Before long Bob's frenzied efforts bore strange fruit. He persuaded the leading Stockholm daily, *Dagens Nyeter,* to publish a series of "maxims," pithy quotes he had collected in a notebook for future use in his plays. A smaller weekly paper published an interview he'd solicited in which he railed against Western decadence and praised Swedish enlightenment. Getting the articles translated into English, he took copies to producers considering *The Parasite,* hoping to steamroll them into offering him a contract. On the heels of my book deal, he was obsessed with the need to quickly get a deal of his own.

By mid-August, he hit pay dirt. The Monkbro Theater, a small but prestigious production company, called to say they wanted to put on a Swedish version of *The Parasite* that winter. Bob reacted oddly. Instead of the joy we felt at his victory, he was depressed.

"The Royal Dramatic Theater is really the best place for my debut," he mused. "The Monkbro is second-level stuff.

I'll just stall Monkbro and use them to leverage the others."

He got on the phone and began calling around. I happened to hear one of his exchanges. ". . . and now you have to make up your mind to sign a contract for this play, time won't wait for you," he warned. "If you don't grab it now, you may lose it!"

He listened briefly, then his tone softened. "No, I'm not threatening you. I just wanted to clarify your position. Yes, I'll call you later, then . . . no, no *I'll* call *you* . . . well, all right then." He hung up and sat there muttering, "The fools. They seem to be everywhere."

We tried to interest him in seeing the Stockholm sights, but no matter where we went he was like a broken record, scheming how to handle one producer or another and continuing to stall the Monkbro people. As August turned to September, his options narrowed. When Monkbro insisted he conclude a firm deal with them, he quibbled over terms and made such outrageous demands the mere fact they kept calling was clear proof they liked *The Parasite* enough to suffer his indignities.

Our own emotional life was stormy too. Quarrels had become so commonplace we'd squabble wherever we were. These angry exchanges almost always focused on trivialities—who said what to whom, or whose memory was more reliable when recounting a shared experience. Juneau often had her feelings hurt in these disputes. They came to be a standing joke among our friends, who good-naturedly nicknamed us "The Battling Chagalls."

The day finally came when we had to leave Lidingo, since Nina Lagergren was due back from Spain. With our limited savings plus the book advance, we could look for another place in Stockholm and stay afloat six months at best—or ship across the Kattegat to Denmark where lower prices would stretch our money a full year. With *Diary* not due out until March, we opted for Denmark. Out of compassion, we invited Bob to join us—and hoped he would not take us up on our offer.

Instead he found a room in town, assuring us he would

soon be inviting us to his grand opening night. Leaving him with a jarful of grass, we last saw him at the train station shaking a victory fist as we headed south to Helsingborg and the ferry that would take us to Copenhagen.

4

Beware the Norsemen's Fury!

spergaerde in Danish means "Garden of Hope," an irony we were soon to appreciate. Renting the main floor of a big house in the modest beach town of Espergaerde—just south of Elsinore's Kronborg Castle where Hamlet lived—we soon learned why the Danish prince was so melancholy.

As autumn deepened and the days grew short, an eerie fog shrouded the coast. The gloom became so intense we were drawn to reading books that matched the weather—macabre tales, satanic novels, and shark attacks—and when snow sheeted the streets, we moved to ghost stories, Aleister Crowley, and other creepy writings. Juneau filled her days sculpting while I struggled with my writing. Evenings we read weird literature and searched the short-wave radio bands for American and English language broadcasts.

Trading weekly letters with Bob, we learned how the Monkbro people had finally wearied of his antics. They insisted he sign a contract with them or break off negotiations, but Bob was still not ready to commit. He aimed to give the Royal Dramatic people "one more effort" before he reluctantly signed with Monkbro. He could "afford to play the waiting game," he wrote, since our friends in Philadelphia—members of his self-styled "sucker list"—continued to send him generous monthly checks.

His next letter was less hopeful. After he threatened the Monkbro Theater once too often, they finally told him to "go with our blessings to the Royal Dramatic, if they want you so badly." Shaken, he began retracing my footsteps. Visiting the two Stockholm publishers who had turned down *Diary,* he offered them his own unpublished novel, warning them "not to make the same big mistake with Robert Summers as they had with David Chagall." He referred to everyone as "fools, idiots, and imbeciles," as the anger behind his words seethed off his pages.

Frozen by the looming prospect of a first book publication, I found it impossible to work on a new novel. So I spent my time typing detailed journal entries and elaborate excursions into Freudian self-analysis, probing my feelings, childhood hurts, and relationship with Juneau. We continued to argue constantly—I, angered at her "unyielding attitude"; she, defending against a "crushed spirit." Time passed slowly as if battling through the foggy skies and frequent drizzles. We found daily solace in the astrology column of our *Herald Tribune,* cheered by the ever-flattering Scorpio and Virgo entries. On rare clear days, we would bicycle three kilometers to the local movie theater, less often the six kilometers to the Louisiana art museum, or—as on two occasions—the grueling hundred-kilometer round trip to Copenhagen.

One evening Juneau's brother called. He was visiting Denmark on a buying trip for his Scandinavian furniture store in Seattle. Johannes, his supplier, suggested he invite us to a dinner party at a downtown Copenhagen nightclub. Late the next afternoon a Mercedes pulled up outside the house. We piled in and Johannes—slim, middle-aged, and charming—enlivened the half-hour drive by chatting about the war years under German occupation.

Our destination was the Capri Nightclub, modeled on French cabarets. We were joined there by a quiet middle-aged couple: Felix played first violin for the Royal Philharmonic, and his wife taught piano and reared their three kids. Voluminous food and drink kept us entertained, along with variety acts introduced by a turbaned Egyptian spieling four languages badly all at the same time.

After the other couple left early, Johannes talked about cultural values and why, as a rich businessman, he felt duty bound to honor musicians, artists, and writers who were grossly underpaid for the meaning they gave to human life. His attitude reflected a widespread Scandinavian view. Writers there carry the honored title "Forfatter" before their last name just as a Ph.D "Doctor" and a college teaching "Professor" does here to compensate for a normally modest income. In this country, as captives of the "best-seller syndrome," we glorify popular hacks writing horror stories or soap opera novels simply because their books make so much money.

That evening was a bright star in what was to be a long gray stretch of isolation. In mid-October, the postman brought a letter from Bob that lit a bomb under our friendship. Explaining how he had undergone a great spiritual change, he was now living a "Poem of Life." This required him to treat every man and woman on earth as characters in a play he was constantly writing. "At all times I speak to everyone in the gentlest, most loving way possible. . . . and use no threats to see other producers or publishers. In short, I submit myself as an Incarnate Idea. . . . it is only I who must justify myself, not they."

He stated his intention to visit my editor to "confess our collusion in coming to Sweden to advance our careers. I shall also tell Mr. Lofgren that I hold immoral the altering of your title *An Experience* to *Diary of a Deaf Mute* so as to increase sales. I believe you owe him an apology, for this and for any other lies you or I may have told.

"I want to tell you also that I am extremely happy I did not receive a contract before I saw this clarity. I was not yet ready to receive a contract. I am trying my very utmost to search my soul to its very roots. I honestly believe that I am now using my titanic will in a proper way, trying so hard to groom myself for the role which I know shall be mine. Love, Bob."

It didn't take great insight to see Bob's "Poem of Life" as a sugar-coated back-stabbing assault against my "success"— my contract, my publisher, and my credibility. His monstrous ego could not bear to be second in anything, so he intended to destroy my publisher's confidence in my book, its title and its author—all in the name of "love, honesty, and the Incarnate Idea." Like a thwarted child who couldn't get what he wanted, he was making sure I wouldn't get it either. My response was quick and direct. I warned him to stay away from my publisher and play his "Poem of Life" games with his own contacts but to leave mine alone.

Though we exchanged several more letters, he never once admitted what I knew to be true in my heart—that he'd already carried out his dirty business with my publisher. My last letter begged him to forsake his so-called poem, pointing out it was just a flimsy excuse to continue exploiting and hurting others for the sake of his bloated ego. "If you choose to be holier than me, do it at your own expense, not mine," I wrote. "Have you shared your new philosophy of absolute honesty with the Sucker List paying your expenses?"

That last line got his attention. Because he obviously feared I was about to write our friends and undermine his source of income—which he undoubtedly would have done had our situations been reversed—his next letter confessed his own "cunning and the measure of terror" my words had struck in his heart. "I am afflicted with power-disease, just as Hitler, Napoleon, and Caesar. I ask you to understand, however, that I in no way begrudge you your contract."

I stopped writing him.

A month later a Swedish friend informed us Bob had been arrested. In his zeal to get a contract, he'd sent a telegram to producer Lars Schmidt—then married to film star Ingrid Bergman—demanding that Schmidt meet him outside a downtown Stockholm cafe, bring along a contract for *The Parasite,* or face dire consequences. When Bob showed up to keep his date with Schmidt, the police were waiting. After an overnight stay in a police cell, they sent him to the state mental facility in Uppsala.

When we called Uppsala, the administrator told us Bob's condition had stabilized and they had discharged him. Acting swiftly, the Swedish government paid his air fare back to family and friends in Philadelphia before he caused them any more trouble.

Two months later, my book came out in Swedish translation—with a changed title. Instead of *En Dovstom's Dagbok* (Swedish for *Diary of a Deaf Mute*), the words *Fangad i Flykten* were inscribed on its cover—Swedish for *Caught in Flight*. Bob and his "Poem of Life" had had the last laugh.

Under whatever title, the book was reviewed everywhere and enthusiastically praised as a "modern classic," "a wonderful book." "We have every reason to be glad this book debuted in Sweden." One reviewer even compared it favorably to the writings of August Strindberg, the much-revered, long-dead playwright. I'd achieved what a Swedish editor friend jokingly called "being world famous in Stockholm." Despite its critical acclaim, the book sold modestly, adding little to our dwindling savings.

One afternoon I was out in the yard watering the marijuana plants when suddenly I felt a sharp pain in my chest followed by partial paralysis of the legs. I was sure I'd been hit simultaneously by a heart attack plus polio, but our local doctor diagnosed a bad case of shingles. My nerves were so shot I couldn't even sit still to read for more than thirty minutes at a stretch, let alone do any useful writing. Reduced to a sniveling, complaining wreck, I felt cowardly and worthless. My self-esteem hit rock bottom.

When the spring thaw came, we harvested our potted pot, packed our clothes and hi-fi, and slept on the deck of an overnight ferry carrying us across the North Sea to England.

◆

The train dumped us out at London's Charing Cross Road, a seedy district near Soho, housing unskilled laborers, transient seamen, and $1.50 prostitutes. With exactly $25 worth of English money in our pockets, we hauled our stuff through the streets until we found bed-and-breakfast lodging at a rundown rooming house where the wallpaper hung down in shreds, big cracks highlighted the plaster, and the only blanket on the bed had a huge burn hole in the center. One thing recommended it—it cost $14 weekly, payable in advance. That left us $11, $4.60 of which we spent for dinner at a nearby cafeteria.

The next morning the landlord served us breakfast in our room—two slices of stale bread fried in lard, which we washed down with a great mug of milky tea. We were so hungry the stuff tasted delicious. After wolfing it down, we went looking for a pawnshop. Juneau had volunteered to sacrifice her diamond engagement ring for the cause, and, too desperate to haggle, we took $46 for a $500 gem. I put on my best suit, kissed her good-bye, and boarded the tube heading downtown to look for work. It was a crazy thing to do since I had no work visa, no money, no visible means of support, and no prior job offer to keep us from being deported as vagrant aliens.

But the Lord shows mercy to idiots. Within a week I landed an editorial job with an electronics journal, redeemed Juneau's ring, found a flat in Knightsbridge—an upscale neighborhood near Harrod's Department Store—and said good-bye to our dingy Charing Cross dungeon. Our new home was a crazy basement apartment with an icy damp bathroom under the sidewalk. Though we paid hefty rent, we were charged with stoking and tending the house's coal-burning furnace set smack in the middle of our living room.

The job brought contacts with other writers, and I soon began selling free-lance articles and book reviews to British magazines. Someone recommended me to a literary agent named James Kinross, a gentle, scholarly Scot, who quickly found a publisher for my long-completed novel *The Century God Slept*. As apparent frosting on the cake, Juneau became pregnant. Yearning for a child of her own, back in Philadelphia she'd gone to a doctor specializing in conception problems. After she'd endured three months of treatment, he assured us we would be able to have a baby. It took a full eighteen months for his words to come true.

Rejoicing over the prospect of our first child, we began putting aside baby things. Two months into her pregnancy, we were listening to BBC radio one night when Juneau suddenly clutched her stomach and groaned.

"What's the matter?" I asked.

"Just a gas pain." She smiled past the agony. "It's already going away."

She took an antacid and I forgot about it. But the pain struck again during the night so we slept in bits and snatches. The next morning she insisted I go to work. When I got back that evening, she had a hot water bottle clutched to her stomach and a robe over her lap. Knowing Juneau would rather bite the bullet than complain, I was really scared and suggested we see a doctor. But she assured me she'd be all right—it was only a stomach flu that would pass in a few days. I loaded her up on aspirin, and that night she seemed to sleep better. But I may have been so tired I slept more heavily and thus did not hear her agonies. In the morning she claimed she felt better and even made breakfast, so I spent the day at work feeling more secure.

When I came home, one look at her pale pain-racked face told me it was no mere stomach flu. This time when I said I was taking her to a doctor, she cried but did not protest. I called the number assigned to us by the National Health Service, and I got an answering service, who advised I call after eight the next morning. Battling to convince the operator this was a real emergency, I finally extracted the doctor's home number.

Dr. Pierce was irritated at being disturbed after working hours, but he gave me directions to his place and we flagged a taxi outside. As I helped my hobbling wife into his home office, the doctor's expression changed from annoyance to grim concern. Hoisting Juneau up on a table, he thumped her abdomen, asked where it hurt, took her temperature, pulse, and blood pressure, then picked up the phone and dialed out.

"This is an emergency," he said. "Get an ambulance here as soon as you can."

He tried to reassure us it was just a precautionary move. But we knew better. The ambulance ride to St. George's Hospital went quickly, though seeing Juneau on a stretcher with attendants fussing around her was no great morale booster. When we arrived at the emergency entrance, they wheeled her away and sent me to the admissions desk where

I numbly filled out forms. Then a nurse led me to a tiny room with painted green walls where I was to spend a long night of anxious agony.

Juneau remembers her thoughts at the time . . .

After so long a wait, was my pregnancy now to be complicated with appendicitis? Instead, the surgeon diagnosed an ectopic or tube pregnancy. Even as I went to the operating room, I would not believe that I would lose that little baby. I asked the surgeons to please transplant the embryo to the right place. I did not know that the fight was for my very life. I had been bleeding internally for many days.

As David waited in the hall outside the surgery room, the anesthesiologist came out to tell him it was touch and go: I might not recover.

I came out of it barely alive. Forty days and forty nights in the hospital and I still came home hardly able to walk. I felt I had sinned. I had tried to change my own destiny. God had punished me by almost taking my life and taking away my wee babe.

I was angry with God. I was depressed. During my recuperation, there were times when I wanted to kill myself. Even the "good" days were bleak and hopeless. I seemed to be smothered in a dark spiritual cloud, and life did not seem worthwhile. The doctors were not able to help the pain, depression, physical weakness, and helplessness I felt. I needed spiritual guidance but didn't know how to pray or to whom. A priest came to my bed in the ward, but his backward collar frightened me and I waved him away.

After I got out of the hospital, I was sitting in Hyde Park one day, and began a chance conversation with a matronly looking lady. As she told me about the Spiritualist Society, her voice became almost a whisper. Looking around, she said, "Mustn't let anyone hear; people don't approve of this." She told me that they gave healing treatments for a small donation at the society offices.

We found a telephone listing for the Spiritualist Society of Greater London, and Juneau made an appointment with a spiritual healer. The society was located in an old brick building near the British Museum. The anterooms looked like something out of a carnival haunted castle, with paneled walls covered by photos of famous mediums. Foggy ectoplasm flowed from their mouths, nostrils, and chests. Seance trumpets, cymbals, and bells were strung like trophies from the ceiling, and the only living person in sight was an elderly, unsmiling woman who seemed to disappear into the woodwork once she'd asked our business.

As we studied the strange adornments, a plump middle-aged woman emerged from an inner room and beckoned Juneau inside. I was left alone to wonder what was happening to her.

> The woman sat me down on a hard wooden bench with fifteen other people, where I waited nervously for my name to be called. About an hour later, I was ushered through a short hall to a small brightly lit room. A plain-looking middle-aged lady sat quietly in a chair with another woman standing beside her who gestured me to the empty chair facing them. The woman who had led me in stood behind me.
>
> I was scared and blurted, "I've been sick . . ."
>
> "Please don't talk," the standing lady interrupted. "Mrs. Phelps has an American Indian guide. He gives her the information, and she will tell you what she learns from the other side."
>
> Mrs. Phelps took my two hands in hers and began to speak as she looked directly into my eyes. "You have been in the hospital, and we came very close to losing you. You were a very sick woman. There was a tiny baby that was too anxious and began to be formed before it reached the right place. It caused dangerous conditions and much blood." She paused. "My guide is finished. Thank you." Her voice trailed off.
>
> The woman behind me took my arm and led me

out. *I couldn't believe what I had just heard. And what a strange way to describe an ectopic pregnancy: "too anxious."*

We went past curtained cubicles into a partitioned room with a padded table where I was asked to wait. This time I was left alone. After a while a woman entered and asked me to remove my coat and shoes and lie on the table. As she worked, she described what she was doing. By holding her hands over my body, she explained, energy would leave her hands and enter my body to help heal it. With my eyes closed, I felt tingling in the parts of my body below where she held her hands. She never touched me but kept her hands an inch or so away.

"You might think that my energy would be depleted by doing this, but the reverse is true," she told me. "I look forward to coming here to give treatments because I always feel so energized afterward."

She passed her hands over me for about half an hour. Then I was dismissed and asked to return weekly.

Now, *I thought,* I should really be healed with both physical doctors and spirits working to help me.

A month later, I was in bed contemplating suicide. My skin was crawling in pain. I was so sensitized to everything that touched me that the only way out of the agony seemed to be by renting a tenth floor hotel room and splattering myself against the pavement far below. Even imagining it was comforting.

Looking back, I realize now who was in control of my life, even how I had invited those fallen angels into my being to take charge through fear and self-loathing. At the time, though, I was sure they were obviously good spirits yearning only for my recovery and spiritual growth. I knew they had to be good because they wanted to heal me. Bad spirits, I'd read, have raucous natures, play childish tricks, and are not too bright.

When troubles come, they come in droves. Late one afternoon, soon after Juneau's return from the hospital, our landlady, Mrs. Bradley, came downstairs while I was at work. She found Juneau reading with a blanket across her lap, and quietly told her we had to get out within the next few days; her cousin was coming to visit for Christmas and she would need the space. Evidently, Juneau's illness had triggered the eviction since we'd paid our rent promptly, did not entertain outsiders, and tended her furnace faithfully. Some folks just can't stand to be reminded of their own mortality, I guess. Moving at any time is a hassle, but when you've just come out of a life-threatening siege, it's pure hell.

Stifling hatred for Mrs. Bradley, I began making the rounds. Everywhere I went, the only flats available were going for rents far too rich for my editor's salary. As a temporary solution, we found a bed-sitting accommodation in Paddington's Talbot Square, at the less desirable north end of Hyde Park. We were located just across the street from the Barington Plaza Hotel, and our neighbors were mostly young literary and show-business types keeping the lid on expenses.

Our digs resembled the movie set of *The L-Shaped Room*. The living area was a fifteen-by-twenty-foot bedroom/sitting room, with a tiny bathroom crammed into space where a closet once stood. We shared a communal toilet with other tenants, down a flight of stairs. Juneau did all her cooking on a single-burner gas hot plate and washed dishes in the bathroom sink. There was no refrigerator, so we limited shopping to what we'd eat during the next twenty-four hours.

We planned to stay there no more than a week until we found something more suitable. We stayed two years. Adding insult to indignity, rent was $28 a week—over 40 percent of my salary, which was considered high by 1960s British standards.

It was the first Saturday in our flat. We kept our windows closed against the incessant banging of construction down on the street below. Suddenly, we heard bellowing male voices. My street-trained ears told me a fight was breaking out, so I raised the window for a better look. A tall, wire-haired man gesticulated wildly as three burly workers crowded in on him. Recognizing a New York accent behind the curses, I took the stairs two at a time to prevent mayhem. I got there just in time.

"You been banging, banging for days!" the American shouted. "Don't you know you're driving us nuts?"

"Easy it goes, or I'll put you down properly," the stoutest worker said.

"Easy? I'll break your hammers. I'll bomb your bulldozers! Don't tell me easy!"

Moving in tight on the angry Yank, the Brits raised their fists to do some business.

"You need a good clout, laddie!" one yelled.

"Hold on," I said.

They all stopped and looked at me oddly.

"My friend here has had a bit much to drink," I said, taking the New Yorker's arm. "If he's offended anyone, I apologize for him."

The workers seemed mollified.

"And knock that noise off!" my new friend yelled, not realizing his good fortune. "My . . ."

I poked him in the chest to get his attention.

"If you want to stay alive, you better get out of here," I hissed in his ear. "These boys will pound you to shreds!"

That sobered him, and he moved off with me. Suddenly, a boyish grin lit up his face, and he put out his hand.

"Hey, pal, thanks," he said. "From one Yank to another."

That was our introduction to Hal Galili, who got the word out that an American writer and his wife had moved into the square. Over the next few days neighbors dropped by to say hello. There was Sally Belfrage, a young Marxist writer, who had just published her first book, *A Room in Moscow*, with lots of notoriety and excellent reviews. The daughter of McCarthy hearings figure, "Hollywood 10" screenwriter Cedric Belfrage (now Comintern Bureau Chief in Cuernavaca, Mexico), Sally had spent eighteen months as a guest student in the Soviet Union and unsurprisingly found that she'd "seen the future and it works." Her brother Nicolas, less enamored of Marxian utopias, spent his days attending the London School of Economics while dreaming of one day writing literary novels a la James Joyce.

Hal Galili, a New York actor who played an Israeli freedom fighter in the film *Exodus,* rented a room from the Belfrages. After ten months on an Israeli kibbutz, he'd had a nervous breakdown and was now in London undergoing LSD-enhanced psychotherapy. Always bubbling over and spouting words faster than his tongue allowed, spurred on by amphetamines and booze, Galili preached the gospel of lysergic acid years before Timothy Leary would ride the drug to worldwide notoriety.

A frequent visitor was writer Kathy Perutz from Long Island, who'd just debuted with a Radcliffe-based novel called *The Perfumed Garden.* Working on a second novel, Kathy launched romances with anyone who might help her "make it big," thrived on gossip about the literary high and mighty, and fought a mostly losing battle against rich foods and pastries.

British actor Chuck Julian filled out the regulars. Chuck had spent a year at a Florida military school and spoke with a New York accent, though he came from a wealthy London family and was a graduate of Winston Churchill's school, Harrow. His latest movie, *The War Lovers,* showcased him as a young navigator who died tragically. Constantly dating show girls in spiked heels towering a foot above his slender five-five, Chuck was shocked over our brazenly growing potted marijuana plants on our window ledge. At the time, possessing marijuana in Britain meant long years of prison if you got caught.

Evenings after work and weekends, we'd gather at the Belfrages' expansive five-room flat to drink, smoke pot, and trade gossip of the rich and infamous. Occasionally, we'd be joined by bigger names like Alan Sillitoe and Vanessa Redgrave, who steered our political parlor talk to the need for legalizing drugs, banning the Bomb, liberating women, and—most passionately—vanquishing world imperialism, centered in the U.S. of A. Every now and again Sally would adopt a conspiratorial tone, pass out mimeographed sheets protesting some government policy, and invite us to put our "bodies on the line" at the latest leftist demonstration.

One Sunday morning at 8:05 a knock at our door found us still in bed. I padded over in my pajamas to answer it, and there stood Sally, smiling with an incongruous "action day" glint in her eyes.

"Come, you'll be late for the sit-down," she said.

"What sit-down?"

"The C N D sit-down. I told you about it last week." Sally's style was to intimidate with outright lies. "Lord Russell will be there, Vanessa, Alan, just everybody. It'll be a fun time, I assure you."

"Don't think I can make it," I said.

"Why not?" she asked.

"Because it's not my country, not my political business, and I can't take sides even if I wanted to because I'd be breaking British law."

"Scared, are you?"

I laughed. "Okay. Where and when?"

"We're meeting outside Fortes on the Strand at ten. See you there."

Juneau was still too weak for such escapades, so I left her behind and took the tube to the Strand. When I got to Fortes Cafeteria, Sally, Nick, and a half dozen comrades wearing jeans and work shirts were just finishing breakfast. After a quick cup of tea, we started off to the rally chatting about revolutionary prospects and the social significance of the new "mod" movement just breaking out in Soho. As somewhat less impassioned participants, Nick and I paired off to talk about writing trends.

When we got to Trafalgar Square, it was bulging with weirdly dressed people sporting hair-styles ranging from motley flowing to long, bizarre, and tousled. Impassive bobbies formed a double cordon around the perimeter, and an usher's column of police led into the center from the east entrance. Near Nelson's Column, a loudspeaker blared impassioned diatribes against the Bomb and unholy imperialistic conspiracies. The milling mob soon cut Nick and me off from the others, plunging us into the main throng where we were surrounded by beards and sandals, baby carriages, Salvation Army types wearing beneficent grins, and an occasional bowler-hatted, umbrella-carrying businessman. Shoved about in a human treadmill, ribs jabbed by stray elbows, we attracted both glowers from bearded bohemians and close-up grins from stained British teeth.

Suddenly, an authoritative hiss pierced the air.

"Attention! Attention!" boomed a deep male voice.

The crowd stilled.

"Attention! In precisely ten minutes this square must be emptied by order of the Ministry. Anyone who remains inside the cordon after that time will be subject to immediate arrest. Attention! Attention—" The announcement was repeated.

A conspiratorial buzzing weaved through the mob. A bearded man to our left shouted, "Send the bloody Bomb back to Washington! Out with Yank submarines!" There were answering shouts, and a unison chant rose and swelled: "Ban the Bomb! Ban the Bomb!" Jostling became fierce; shoulder blades and elbows rapped our backs and chests; scattered curses and protests punctuated the Bomb-banning chorale. Up ahead we saw a bobby's truncheon arc out and then heard a dull splot sound and a howl of fear-filled pain. The mob responded by a throaty roar and arms flailed about, accompanied by hooting and booing.

Nick turned a startled face to me. "Let's get the —— out of here," he said.

Needing no more urging, I lowered my shoulder and pushed back the way we'd come. The crowd suddenly reeled back from an assault by horse-mounted bobbies, opening a strip of daylight for our retreat. "You filthy ——," someone screamed in my ear, a fist pounded into my shoulder, and a knee jammed into my thigh. I punched out angrily, and the space reopened, allowing us to slip through and break free onto the sidewalk.

Nursing our bruises, we decided to leave without meeting Bertrand Russell or the rest of the Committee for Nuclear Disarmament's celebrity hosts. It was my first encounter with revolutionary action, a tactic that was destined to cross the Atlantic and enflame America in a few short years.

———————————— ♦ ————————————

Juneau's health improved slowly, and the months turned into our first year. Her legs were still shaky, and she spent most of her days in the bed-sitter, leaving only for daily trips to the grocery shop. Most nights she was too exhausted to even socialize with our friends, so I went next door alone while she stayed home. Obviously, any notion of her taking a job was out of the question.

My work had become burdensome as my boss, Colonel Askew—a retired army officer who thought he was still on the compound—had taken to venting more of his spleen on the resident Yank. His previous whipping boy, Jim Tucker, had gone on to bigger and better things with the BBC, following the footsteps of former staffer Arthur C. Clarke who'd hit a home run with *2001—A Space Odyssey*. As another hireling whose writing ambitions were no secret, I became Tucker's replacement. Stomping out of his frosty-glassed lair, Askew used the occasional editing lapse to humiliate me before my colleagues. A misplaced comma or misspelled proper name would redden his face and neck with apoplectic passion. Slapping the offending galley or manuscript on my desk, he would point his pencil at the cursed spot and hiss disapproval.

"Double-check, triple-check if you have to! But don't you dare send me such examples of wretched editing," he would rail, then stomp out and slam his door behind him.

A few times I found my hands balling into fists. Had we not depended desperately on the bimonthly check, the colonel could easily have earned himself a knuckle massage on his face. Such revenge fantasies helped me ride out Askew's outbursts, but I began to long for release. A note in my journal for that time cried, How long, O Lord? It took three weeks for my plea to be answered.

Late one Thursday in February just before quitting time, I got a phone call from James Kinross.

"I've got some good news," he said. "Jim Knapp-Fisher at Sidgwick and Jackson has had glowing reader reports on *The Century God Slept* and wants to meet you before going ahead."

"Really? Great. When?"

"Call his office tomorrow morning and set up a time." Giving me the number, he rang off and left me in an excited funk.

I shared the news with Juneau after work. *Century* was by far my most daring work. I'd experimented with graphics, using italics, capitals, dreams, poetry, news clips, and a far-out typographical style that challenged the staid traditions of the novel. It couldn't help getting noticed—so we hoped.

Next morning I called Sidgwick and Jackson. Director James Knapp-Fisher was out, but his secretary set up a meeting for the following Monday. The weekend went too slowly, and when we got up Monday morning, rain was pouring down in sheets. It took longer than I'd planned to find their offices, and I arrived ten minutes late, dripping wet.

The place looked like an old paneled mausoleum. Taking my drenched raincoat, the secretary led me to the director's office where a wiry man in his sixties sat behind a huge walnut desk. I went to shake his hand.

"Mr. Knapp-Fisher?" I asked.

"Yes, good," he said, ignoring my palm. "And this is Andrew Dawnay; he's the one who read your book and likes it."

I shook hands with a tall young man who had the reserved confidence of good breeding.

"You've written a great book," he said, smiling. "How long did it take you?"

We spent the next twenty minutes chatting about post-beatnik rebels, British mods, literary trends, and the vagaries of an American education. I warmed to Dawnay who seemed up on what was happening, but I found Knapp-Fisher a somber, if sly, old devil. Finally, Dawnay nodded at the director.

"Fine, then, that's done," Knapp-Fisher said. "We're buying your book, Mr. Chagall. Please tell Mr. Kinross to call me, and we'll work out arrangements."

Floating with exhilaration over to the Strand, I called Kinross from an outdoor telephone kiosk and spent the rest of the day in a rosy haze, barely aware of the articles and galleys that came across my desk. Kinross called at work the next day to say Knapp-Fisher had agreed to a fifty-pound advance and he'd be meeting there to hash out timing and promotion.

"Congratulations. You're with a fine old traditional publisher," Kinross said. "By the by, I don't think I told you. Your editor, young Andrew Dawnay, is also known as Lord Dawnay, son of the duke. He and his cousin Peter are part owners of the firm."

I grinned as I hung up, then tried to share my joy with my co-workers. But they didn't want to hear any of it. Biting my tongue, I realized my success only made them feel more miserably trapped by contrast. Dreams of freedom from wage-earning drudgery were hopes they could not share. Maybe that was Askew's problem as well.

◆

"So what does it actually do?" Sillitoe asked.

"What does it do?" Galili asked incredulously. "It rearranges the molecules of your brain, shakes up your atoms, disintegrates your personality, that's all it does! I wish you could know lysergic acid like I do—it'd do wonders for you, Alan, especially with your writing talent. Wow!"

Six of us shared a bagels-and-tuna salad breakfast at the Belfrages this Sunday morning. Sillitoe, his wife Ruth, Sally Belfrage, Juneau, and I listened to Hal Galili preach the merits of LSD psychotherapy, which he was taking at Harrow-on-the-Hill Hospital. He'd handed out copies of a published study by Dr. Sidney Cohen of UCLA claiming LSD shortened conventional therapy time from several years to a few months. Hal had been on it a month now, and though we hadn't seen any dramatic changes yet, he continually raved of his breakthroughs. My curiosity was aroused by his descriptions of the drug's bizarre effects, which seemed to mimic ecstatic religious experiences. Juneau felt it might help her emotional ills.

"Why don't you get us some to try?" I asked.

"Oh, I couldn't do that," Hal said soberly. "They keep all the vials under lock and key. They only take one out at a time when they're ready to inject it."

"So we're stuck with taking your word for it," said Sillitoe. Alan prided himself for the instinctive skepticism of his working class roots. Before earning a living as a writer, he'd once unloaded produce in the markets.

"That's about it," Hal replied. "But I do have some great pot . . ."

Taking out a cigarette pack, he extracted several joints and lit one that passed around. When it reached Sillitoe, he barely pulled in a whiff of smoke before sending it on. The next time he just pretended to inhale.

Hal noted his aversion. "I've got some uppers you can have, Alan," he offered.

Sillitoe shook his head. "No, thank you. Speed of any kind is antirevolutionary."

"What? How so?" I asked.

"The ruling classes give it to workers so they can stay at their tasks longer and turn out more product. In Peru, it's cocaine for the field hands. In Birmingham, it's amphetamines for the assembly line. Marijuana is okay because it slows things down and mellows the nerves."

"Why didn't you have more, then?" Sally asked mischievously.

Sillitoe cleared his throat. "I'm fighting a cold . . . didn't want to aggravate it. More to the point, what's to be done with the bloody U.S. of A. and their insatiable imperial greed?"

It was a frequent charge by British Marxists. Even the election of John F. Kennedy last year hadn't softened their hatred of America. As usual, we rose to the bait.

"I can't see how an Englishman can call America an imperialist nation," I said. "I mean, we had to drive you blokes off our turf if I read history rightly. What countries have we enslaved recently?"

The next twenty minutes saw us going at it hot and heavy. Neither side gave an inch, and passions were boiling. Convinced of our own rightness, Juneau and I found it hard to understand how these otherwise pleasant people could justify Soviet murders and brutality as 'revolutionary necessities.' But as fists began to clench and teeth to grind, Hal jumped in to lighten things up.

"Anybody for a cheese Danish?" he asked.

Passing the cake around, he managed to break off the tired old argument that never went anywhere or changed anyone's mind. Though Juneau and I didn't deny America's global power and influence, it was simply a question of which superpower—Russia or the U.S.A.—was more benevolent. For us, it was no contest, but for Sally, Alan, and our other Socialist friends, Russia was not only their clear overseer of choice, she was their religion.

5

Rule, Brittania!

L etters from Philadelphia gave sketchy news on old friends. Late one afternoon Dot Summers tried to awaken Bob but found it impossible. He was deep in a drug coma, courtesy of a sleeping pill overdose. Pumped out at the veterans hospital, he spent several months in a psychiatric ward and was now out on the streets again, promoting his plays and hustling after producers in New York. Al DeLeo had quit his waiter's job, shaved his head to become more "holy," and mysteriously disappeared, leaving Wendy with two babies to raise. Davis Grubb had been unable to repeat the success of *Night of the Hunter*, and thwarted ambition drove him over the edge. His brother found him in his apartment, comatose from a drug overdose, seated in a rocking chair, dressed in his dead mother's clothes. Still alive, he was taken to a mental hospital.

At the institution, the colonel turned some of his nastiness toward Bob Milne, but my job grew increasingly more burdensome. With the book not due for another six months, my self-control began to slip after one particularly wretched Friday. I startled Askew by barking back when he snarled, then determined to quit my job and look for another.

"Nothing could be as bad as this one," I told Juneau.

"Yes, it could," she said. "No job at all, for instance."

But when she saw how miserable I was, she agreed with my resolve to leave. Since I had a week's vacation coming up, I decided to give notice when I returned to work good and rested. The colonel, like any jungle beast, was sensitive to the strength of his prey: whenever I felt weak, he attacked, but when I was strong, he went after Milne.

During my time off, Juneau and I visited the Ernest George crematorium in Golders Green where we stared at the small, unimpressive urns containing the ashes of Anna Pavlova and Sigmund Freud. Somehow the insignificance of their final resting place depressed us—the end of all earthly glory in a dull gray pot. Our spirits were restored a bit by corned beef sandwiches at Beziak's Delicatessen, but the tube ride home found both of us in a reflective mood, questioning the real value of fame.

At work, I looked for the right moment to drop my bombshell. Askew was gone the first two days, and the rest of the week, sensing my power, he badgered Milne. Suspense built over the weekend as I yearned to have it over with. It was not until Wednesday of the next week that our moment of truth arrived. Just before lunch, the colonel called me into his office.

"I was looking over those fillers you did yesterday," he began. "They were miserable, Shag-all." He made it sound like "Shag" as in shaggy and "all" to underline the point. "If you ever expect to be any kind of a writer, I have to tell you the outlook is pretty bleak."

"Balderdash!" I shouted.

He stared at me stunned. "What? What's that?"

Feeling anger spilling over, I let go. "I said you're full of balderdash, Askew. You're a petty man who takes out his misery on people who need their jobs too badly to fight back!"

"You're mad," he said. "Get out of here before I teach you a lesson in civility."

Eyes narrowed, he stared at me menacingly and raised his hand as if to strike. A year's worth of frustration erupted as I grabbed his forearm and shoved him against the wall, feeling pleasure as he gasped.

"You lay a hand on me, and I'll lay you out," I said softly. When I let go, his arms went limp, and his eyes would not meet mine. "You've got my three weeks notice."

"That's not proper time," he mumbled. "We'll need to find a replacement. Give us until the end of next month."

He seemed so beaten my passion drained away. "Sure, okay," I said. "I'll stay until the end of July."

"Good!" The colonel brightened, extending his hand. "No hard feelings, I hope?"

"No hard feelings," I said, shaking hands.

When I went through his door and saw the others looking at me quizzically, I grinned, waved and felt as if I were walking on air.

The days flew by. Askew found reasons to send me to Oxford, Rugby, and other towns where he could justify the outlay in the name of electrical news. And when I was in the office, he managed to be out, so we kept happily out of each other's face until that final Friday when I was handed $168 in separation pay and said good-bye forever to the Institution of Electrical Engineers.

Freedom from workplace oppression soon turned to anxiety over money. There was no escaping that ancient human curse demanding we earn our keep by sweating it out, physically or otherwise. I hustled like mad to pull in freelance paychecks, but aside from a few book review assignments and three-dollar letters-to-the editor, pickings were lean indeed. Editing galleys of my book boosted our hopes but put no bread on the table, so we borrowed $200. Juneau began polishing her engagement ring in readiness for the pawnshop, but then providence smiled. After ninety days of unemployment, I landed a staff writing post with AEI Ltd., parent company of Hotpoint and the biggest electrical conglomerate in England.

My first day at work was a revelation. Where the institution had been stuffy and ludicrously self-important, AEI was elegant, classy, and relaxed. Management offices were located at Crown House on the Strand, a glass-and-brown-brick building that exuded understated power. As soon as I reported, I was told that publicity director Hugh Veysey wanted to chat before I got down to business, and since he was out for the day, why didn't I just go home for the weekend? With pay, of course.

On Monday I was assigned a desk in an open office. Piling me up with brochures, sales sheets, and news releases, publications chief Alderton told me to "familiarize myself" with the range of writing I'd be doing. Immediately, I began to feel my electronic inadequacies, a pretentious fraud taking good British money for doing nothing. The insecurity lasted only until some of my fellow writers dropped by to introduce themselves and impress me with their own technical prowess. I soon realized they knew even less than I did, and thanking my stars for a great high-school physics teacher named Dr. Boileau, I picked my spots to astound them with formulae I'd been forced to memorize many years before. Soon I found myself alone and at peace.

The following week when I came to work, a "reorganization" had taken place. I'd been moved to a two-man office, sharing space with two desks, two typewriters, one phone, and a very nervous fifty-two-year-old publicist named Geoff Burdett. Like the others, Burdett tried to intimidate me with his wealth of experience and contacts, hinting he had been paired with me to "take me under his wing." When he began cross-examining me about my time at the institution, I cut him off, and he fell apart.

Confiding how he'd been reduced from his own upstairs office with a private secretary to this two-man editorial team, with house payments due, a family to provide for, and scant prospects elsewhere for a middle-aged burnout, he was at his wit's end to maintain his spirits and sanity. He went on whining this way for the better part of a week, even after Hugh Veysey gave me my first assignment—a training brochure for new recruits in the appliance division. When I found Burdett's complaining prevented my getting on with the job, I told him I'd have to ask for other arrangements if he didn't clam up.

"Oh no, please!" he cried. "Don't do that! I'll keep mum."

After eighteen years with the company, he understood

corporate realities better than I. Now viewed as a worthless hack, Geoff was given no new work assignments as a goad to his seeking another job elsewhere. Meanwhile his paychecks depended on continuing management charity. If no worthwhile work came out of our pipeline, we'd both soon be out on the street. Once he shut up, I was able to work quickly and turn in my copy. A few days later Veysey summoned me into his office. Division chief Sir Arthur Elton stood there as Veysey proceeded to say how pleased he was with my effort, and Sir Arthur added his own complimentary comments. I felt I was off to a good start, which implied we could look forward to a more stable bank balance.

◆

Christmas holidays meant time off from work and traditional carols on TV and radio. As had been the case since grammar-school days, the religious songs moved me to tears and made me feel my unworthiness all the more. But I was a dedicated disciple of Freud, so merely acknowledging my faults was sufficient to forgive them. With diaries and single sheets full of "psychological insights," I was certain I was handling my psychic progress in the prescribed way. "The truth shall set you free" was my favorite saying, while astrology and spiritualism were the closest Juneau and I came to any sort of religion.

Even Marxists were not immune to the spirits. One evening at the Belfrages, Sally brought out a Ouija board.

"Who's game for a round of ghosts?" she asked.

Hal gleefully set up a card table and shoved Chuck into a chair. Nick, David, Sally, and I took places around the table. I was scared. None of us had any experience with this sort of thing, and who knew what kinds of spirits we might contact?

I remembered that my grandmother had used Ouija boards and gone to seances where she sought contact with her dead children she was grieving for.

Who might we raise up? My dead father? David's brother? Or an evil stranger of ill will?

Hal grew serious. "We want to make this a real experiment, so let's all concentrate. No fooling around. We'll just put our fingers lightly on the planchette, and let's have no pushing by anyone. We'll really give this thing a chance to work on its own."

The alphabet circled one side of the board, and Yes and No were printed at the bottom. Each of us placed two fingers of one hand lightly on the pointed marker and closed our eyes in concentration. After a minute, Sally asked, "Who's on the other side?"

No movement. "Maybe using the alphabet is too complicated when we're just starting out," she suggested. "Let's try a yes or no question. How about this—is there anyone here who wants to talk to us?"

We sat quietly touching the floating pointer, eyes closed, listening to our breathing. Still no movement.

"Will I get the movie role I just auditioned for?" Hal asked. The planchette began to move under our fingers. Slowly, it pointed to M, then to G, B, A, T, L, and Z. My fingertips were touching it very lightly, and as it moved my hand had to follow to keep in contact. Suddenly, it stopped.

"All right, who was pushing it around?" David asked accusingly. "Hal—you did it, didn't you?"

Everyone denied having put any pressure on the marker. We all felt an eerie sensation as we folded up the table. "Someone must have been unconsciously pushing it," Nick said. I didn't think so. And I didn't want to play any more.

Meanwhile, production on my book had hit all kinds of roadblocks. First the printer refused to typeset the manuscript, complaining about "profanities and vulgarities" that forced me to rewrite several sections to his tender sensibilities. Then the Dawnays decided against an inspired abstract cover design Juneau had prepared and replaced it with a glossy photographic format depicting a scantily clad female stretching her arms to the skies. They never satisfactorily explained what this had to do with my book, but the upshot was another dart of rejection piercing our already tender hearts. Adding insult to indignity, the various delays finally forced Sidgwick and Jackson to reschedule the publication date from winter to early spring.

The first week of the New Year, art head David Hughes invited me out to lunch. We walked a short distance to The Aldwych, a private club with a doorman, canopy and the richest paneled walls I'd ever seen. Greeting David by name, the manager sat us at a choice table in the dining room where a dozen older men in business suits never seemed to notice us as we took our places.

"The Aldwych is a very special club," Hughes said proudly. "Mostly royalty, wealthy businessmen and a few younger rising stars."

"I'm impressed," I said and was.

Following a sumptuous roast beef luncheon, Hughes got down to business. "What are your plans at AEI?" he asked.

"Plans? Just to do the best job I can and learn to do it even better."

"Hugh likes the way you write and feels you fit well into his plans," he went on. "There's a bright future for you with AEI, David. No doubt in a little while you could move up to Alderton's job or possibly higher. And I could put you forward for membership in The Aldwych Club. I've some clout here I might say, not immodestly."

I was overwhelmed. "I'm really flattered by the confidence you and Hugh have in my work. But I can't give you an answer until I've thought about it and talked it over with my wife."

"I understand completely. Take all the time you need, and we'll talk again."

Hughes stood, he nodded to the manager on the way out, and we walked back to Crown House chatting about everything else except what really mattered. That night Juneau and I talked until 2:00 A.M., digging deeply into our feelings and hopes for the future. I cited the precedent of T. S. Eliot, who brought his family to England and worked as a bank director while writing poetry evenings, weekends, and holidays. We both liked the wide-open British culture, loved London, and were grateful for the acceptance at AEI and for my free-lance efforts.

On the other hand, English wages were low, and I found myself losing the rhythm of American speech, not only in my writing but in ordinary conversation. A similar loss had crept into Eliot's poetry, which conceptually and in word patterns became more and more British as he moved into middle age. Since the election of John F. Kennedy, America seemed to be experiencing a cultural renaissance, and there was a patriotic pull to be there for the "New Frontier." Finally, if we stayed it would mean seeing our families only on the rare occasion of a trans-Atlantic trip.

When we finally closed discussion to go to sleep, we were no closer to a decision than when we started.

◆

Work settled into a blur of routine meetings, lunches, and occasional spurts of writing. During the many doldrum hours, I read library books on psychology and the occult while Burdett gabbled incessantly, battling boredom and blowing off anxiety.

Late one afternoon while thumbing through *The Mediumship of Jack Webber,* I came across a remarkable photo of Webber seated in a chair, eyes closed in trance, while out of his nostrils streamed long strands of milky ectoplasm. It was my chance to pay Burdett back for his verbal pollution.

"Look here, Geoff," I called.

"What is it?" Burdett asked grumpily.

"You're always pooh-poohing psychic research and spiritual things. Well, just take a look at this."

Placing the book on his desk, I waited as he looked it over. His nose wrinkled, his eyes narrowed and he frowned.

"What in the world are you showing me here?" he asked.

"Ectoplasm. That's the stuff coming out of his nose."

"Ectoplasm? Uuuugghhhhh—disgusting!" Slamming the cover closed, he shoved the book back at me as I laughed. "You've a strange sense of humor, I must say!"

So went the off hours at a multinational corporate giant. Meanwhile, Kathy Perutz's book came out, and I followed her reviews closely, hoping to learn what effect they had on sales. While consoling her on the bad ones and cheering the good coverage, I found myself agreeing with the typically British assessment printed in *John O'London:* ". . . lightly amusing, sometimes schmalzy tale of a young American girl who has to grow up in the end, excellent for trains, lost weekends and the odd bout of flu." There was a strain of jealousy, too, since Sally Belfrage had gotten Kathy an American publisher two weeks after she signed with the British publisher, but she never once offered to help me. Alan Sillitoe added his support with a quote praising *Garden* as a "fresh and fascinating novel" while never once showing any interest in reading *The Century God Slept*. Adding fire to the rivalry darkening my heart, my Swedish publisher wrote they were remaindering *Diary*, underlining it as a commercial flop.

Looking back, I realized I'd never been helped or encouraged by left-wingers or beatniks. All my boosts in England, and Sweden as well, had come from aristocrats and establishment people. For the son of a grocery salesman, it was a sobering thought.

The somber mood lasted only until lunch the next day when Vic Briggs, editor of a paperback trade monthly, told me Panther Books was seriously considering taking on my book. Panther was a classy reprint firm that published George Orwell, Jack London, and Arthur Koestler. Though hope stirred in my heart, I squelched it, afraid to risk another letdown as in Sweden.

Monday morning Andrew Dawnay called at work. Thomas Yoseloff of A. S. Barnes was in town, had read *Cen-*

tury over the weekend, loved it, and wanted American rights. Offering a token $250 advance, he proposed making it up with sliding royalties that would pay me handsomely if the book took off when released in New York next year. A meeting was set up for Thursday at Sidgwick and Jackson, and though having the book come out in America was a dream come true, I determined to hold out for a bigger advance.

Thursday morning was typically London in late winter. A thick fog shrouded the gray cloud cover, and a mist continually watered the streets, though no raindrops fell. Arriving early, I built up a twenty-minute head of steam waiting in Knapp-Fisher's office for Yoseloff, who came ten minutes late. He was short, quiet-sneaky, wore a pinstriped suit, and was very New Yorky. My first reaction was distrust.

The moment Knapp-Fisher introduced us all, I blurted out, "I can't accept your offer. I'm looking for a $1,000 advance."

Everyone stared at me with stunned expressions, hardly believing what they'd heard. Andrew recovered first, urging me to reconsider, even as Yoseloff pointed out some non-monetary advantages he could offer—the personal attention of a smaller firm, a prestige imprint, full author participation at every stage of the publishing process, including advertising and promotion. But when it came to the advance, he was adamant. After a full hour going back and forth with neither of us budging, Yoseloff stood.

"I want to be frank with you," he said. "In twenty-two years in the business, I've never had this happen to me before. But I'm a reasonable man. I'll be in town another week in case you change your mind."

When he left, Andrew took me to a nearby coffee shop where he spent another thirty minutes urging me to change my mind. But I was persuaded that if too little money were invested up front, the publisher would be tempted to spend too little to push it. The next afternoon Andrew called at AEI again, advising me to accept Yoseloff's offer. It was only after I held fast that he told me Panther Books had bought British reprint rights for a $420 advance.

That evening Juneau and I celebrated with a fish-and-chips dinner. Oddly enough, the paperback sale to Panther weakened rather than strengthened our resolve. After staying up to 3:00 A.M. hashing it out, we decided to settle for $500. Relieved that the thing was settled, I called Dawnay. He acted disinterested and said he would discuss my compromise offer with Knapp-Fisher and call back that afternoon. He didn't. The next morning I called him to learn Yoseloff would not budge from his original offer. So I called Yoseloff at his hotel. He sounded an intransigent note but agreed to meet me the next evening.

When I got to the Westbury Hotel, he greeted me warmly, and I was a lot less cocky, which helped matters enormously.

"You're a gifted writer," he said. "and you've written a remarkable book in *The Century God Slept*. But I caught some faulty grammar, typos, and misspellings. If you can meet me here Friday, I'd like to go over the manuscript with you."

"I'd love to," I said. "But there's another matter . . ."

"Yes?" His eyes glinted defensively, expecting me to bring up the advance.

"The British printer insisted I edit out some stuff that really should be in there. I'd like to see it back in the American edition."

"Consider it done," he said. "The English tend to be more thin-skinned than we are. With today's obscenity standards as they are, I'm sure your mild material would be beyond reproach. Do we have a deal, then?"

"We have a deal."

We shook hands and he smiled. "I like you, David, so I'll add $100 to the advance. I'll make it $350, okay?"

I smiled, glad the jousting was ended. "Thanks," I said. And meant it.

Home was a more relaxed place as our hearts yearned westward toward America. After three years abroad, it would feel good to hear the homey sounds of southern drawls and New York growls again. Although the job at AEI and its Aldwych Club future were powerful lures, Juneau and I agreed our destinies lay with the land of our birth.

———————————————————— ♦ ————————————————————

As the April publication date neared, trade ads and publicity put out by Sidgwick and Jackson raised our spirits and our social standing in the lit set. We were invited to more parties, where our opinions were welcomed and even got occasional approval, despite our openly pro-American bias.

At work, the secret knowledge we would soon be going home promoted a devil-may-care ease that protected me in the pecking-order warfare that goes on in every office. Geoff Burdett, suffering ever increasing humiliation as a nonproductive freeloader, ranted and raved about everyone else's inadequacies or told endless stories of the glory days when his star was on the rise. Though I felt sorry for the guy, his yapping drove me nuts and when it prevented my doing any effective work, I began leaving the office early just to get free.

One day after lunch, I stopped into a bookshop on the Strand and picked up *The Bookseller* trade magazine. The inside front pages carried two full-page ads from Sidgwick and Jackson—one for John F. Kennedy's *When England Slept,* the other for *The Century God Slept* trumpeting, "The book every one is talking about! Some people love it, others hate it, one printer refused to print it!" Floating on air until quitting time, I felt being paired with JFK was undoubtedly prophetic.

The day before the book's official publication date of April 6, our dreams yielded to the real world of critics and cranks. Anthony Burgess of *Clockwork Orange* fame began the assault with a *Yorkshire Post* review that carped about my "chunks of italic and hysterical upper case, all very childish" prose. That same day's *Daily Mail* saw it "written on a rubber typewriter by a young novelist who does not know how to erase. . . . recommended purely as proof that to be hip is not enough."

Before we could find a hole to hide away, the influential *Sunday Times* found nicer things to say: "Chagall has written a serious 'beat' book, with talent, warmth and a great deal of decency. Lots of 'experimental' writing, like suddenly

PRINTING A SENTENCE IN CAPITAL LETTERS, or using a series of
short phrases
on separate lines
or *printing certain passages in italics.*"

Over the next two weeks, as Juneau and I haunted bookshops, rearranging displays and counting sales, fine reviews appeared in the *Western Mail, Daily Worker,* and *Topic,* the British newsweekly magazine, versus a bad one in the *Tribune.* All told it scored what the business calls mixed reviews, which unhappily dampened my publisher's enthusiasm even though the entire first printing quickly sold out. With the Panther reprint due out the following spring, they decided to bank their profits and not risk another printing. The wind out of our sails, our hearts turned toward home.

A few days later I gave notice at AEI. Veysey called me into a late afternoon conference. Afterward he invited me out for a drink with his assistant, Ivan Hooper, and we went to the nearby Waldorf Hotel, settling in at a barside table around a bottle of French wine.

"Here's to good fellows," Veysey said, lifting his glass. After a short pause, he looked me straight in the eye. "So you're bound and determined to leave us, Shag?"

I nodded. "It's time I went home."

"Can't say we're happy about that," Veysey said. "We had quite a few big plans for you, you know."

"I appreciate it, Hugh. This is the best job I've ever had, and you're the most decent people I've ever worked with. Believe me when I say our decision didn't come easy."

"What's the big attraction over there anyway?" Hooper asked.

"Well, it's my country for a start," I replied. "And it's where the action is now, since you folks have handed over the job of keeping the world free. That's no easy thing, and it's not easy living in America. Life here is much more pleasant, the British people are a lot more human and relaxed. And more civilized, too."

"But," said Veysey.

"Yes, but—but my place is there. That's where the fight will be decided, one way or the other. If the light goes out there, it goes dark all over the world."

Veysey smiled. "I understand perfectly, old Shag," he said. "Good luck, and we'll miss you."

Lifting our goblets, we toasted jolly old England, America the beautiful, and each other one last time. Then we went our separate ways.

♦

The last few weeks were filled with dumb details. I finished off lagging projects at work, and we sold our hi-fi to two young men from the provinces. Then we gave away our bicycles, leaving that much less to drag back. We took passport photos, set up an appointment at the U.S. Embassy, and booked passage on the *Queen Mary* sailing June 7.

Days blurred into one another, memorable only for odd snatches—a restful Bach concert at Royal Festival Hall, good-bye lunches with British friends, and a short chat with Andrew Dawnay who, just before he ran off to "dress a window in Mayfair," told me *The Century God Slept* had just been banned in South Africa. The news cheered my anti-apartheid soul.

As departure loomed closer, I felt my heart grow softer, more yielding, less fearful of attracting attacks by its vulnerability. As Geoff Burdett sensed the inevitability of losing my sympathetic ear, his complaints and moaning grew more intense and desperate. When the final Friday arrived, we shook hands and wished each other luck. Juneau managed to sell a stack of LPs to a Soho shop for $30, and we enjoyed a fine seafood lunch on part of the proceeds.

Our last Saturday in London, Chuck Julian took us to the Drury Lane Theater where he'd gotten us front row seats for a new musical play, *Stop the World, I Want to Get Off!* starring Anthony Newley. We were so enchanted and excited, we couldn't stop talking about the show well into the early morning hours.

Wednesday afternoon. Strolling a last time to Hyde

Park, we listened to a preacher threaten the wrath of God at Speaker's Corner and marveled at the incredible blue-green of the grassy expanse siding the Serpentine where young lads sailed their boats. We stopped off at the Belfrages for last good-byes. Sleeping came hard that night as we began missing things British and the wonderful, eccentric island we had called home.

Then came the taxi, the train, and the deep blue sea.

6

◆

You Can't Go Home Again

Landing in New York was like visiting a foreign country. The city's frantic pace and rude gabble assaulted our nervous systems like a symphony orchestra run amuck. Clearing customs and checking our baggage through to Philadelphia, we boarded the train at Pennsylvania Station and listened to the sad clackety clack of the railroad tracks until a station sign told us we were back in the City of Brotherly Love.

We were overjoyed to find Patti and Ronny waiting on the platform with our dog, Sarah, and we all took a cab back to their apartment, where we spent hours filling one another in on three years of changes. Their warm reception raised our expectations of getting a hero's welcome home. But that lasted only until the next afternoon when we walked over to Rittenhouse Square and found the old coffee shop characters encamped on benches.

No one even looked up as we approached until Center City Sonny, a fortyish hipster, glanced across, nodded lazily and resumed listening to an apocryphal drug story being told by a young bearded longhair with a guitar case. Juneau and I waited several minutes for somebody—anybody—to ask where we'd been or even give us a conventional "What's happening, man?" But no one even met our glance. We might as well have just returned from having a milkshake at Day's

Delicatessen instead of thirty-eight grueling months of European adventure.

Across the plaza we spotted Bob Summers sitting on a bench. Holding a slim book in his arm, he was talking intensely with a middle-aged man and sporting a new look. His hair had grayed, and he wore it long and flowing, set off by a rakish scarf flung artistically across his shoulder. His eyes met ours, and he smiled flirtatiously. I smiled back, and he walked over to us.

"Hello," he said. And waited.

"Hello, Bob," we replied. And waited. Nothing more was said. He walked off with a slight wave of his hand, while we lingered a few minutes longer before leaving the square. Not a soul had welcomed us home. But we quickly shed our hurt feelings. More important problems faced us than being ignored by old cronies.

Over the next few weeks while Juneau spent her days looking for an apartment, I looked for work. One evening we were invited over for dinner by friends of the Weingrads. The husband worked as an ad copywriter for a proprietary drug firm while his wife, born in Austria but raised in Switzerland when her wealthy Jewish family fled one step ahead of the Nazi occupation, was a new mother complete with nursemaid and cook. They lived in a converted townhouse they had transformed from shabby decay to paneled opulence, furnishing it with chrome-and-glass tables and varnished cabinetry. Following an elegant presentation of lamb, asparagus, and mint aspic, we settled into easy chairs in the sunken living room, sipped cognac, and lit cigars prior to settling the world's problems.

"So how does all this seem to you after Europe?" Barry asked.

"Very rich," I replied, prompting a frown.

"Yes, of course—but I mean societally. The mantle of power is not an easy one to wear, but the baton has passed to this generation and we've got the obligation to assume it. As I'm sure you'll agree, David, we are the generation of destiny."

At first I thought he was putting me on, but his somber expression told me he meant it.

"You'll have to make allowances for us," I said. "When we left, Eisenhower was president, and college kids were still staging panty raids."

"I understand," he said consolingly. "The New Frontier spirit takes some getting used to, but you and I both know as writers what power is and who has it. We are the new opinion leaders, you and Ron and I—it's up to us to shape the society we want to leave behind for our children. I may spend my days writing on scientific subjects, but I really consider myself a historian. I don't know if Ron told you, but I'm working on a book right now and you can mark my words and remember them—before the sixties are ended, we'll have created a new world that's never been known before, a world of peace, prosperity, and world unification."

"Sounds great," I said. "Let's drink to it."

Clacking glasses, I tried to turn the talk to less cosmic matters, but Barry wouldn't have it. Going on and on in the same grandiose way, he had me half-convinced he had all this power and influence and perhaps it would be to my benefit to join him for the ride. When he asked about my plans, I told him I was looking for a job and—violating a long-standing principle—I allowed him to "arrange" an interview for me with his company, Smith Kline and French Pharmaceuticals.

Two days later I found myself visiting their plant on the outskirts of town, where for half a day I was interrogated by personnel flaks, sneered at by secretaries who held me waiting in paneled reception rooms, and tantalized by smug junior execs ensconced behind their frosty-glassed doors. They kept impressing me with their superiority, the old-family traditions breathing spirit into SKF, and the grand privilege afforded me merely being considered as a potential SKFer. Long before the ordeal ended, I realized I didn't have a chance.

Not only did I lose time, but those institutional hacks succeeded in taking a big bite out of my confidence. That night as I nursed my wounded pride I vowed—like Blanche DuBois in *A Streetcar Named Desire*—to trust in the kindness of strangers rather than ever again follow the self-serving recommendations of "friends."

A bright spot in the struggle to get re-established came one afternoon when I stopped by to see Thomas Yoseloff, in town fulfilling his role as director of University of Pennsylvania Press. After sharing his plans for the American edition of my book, he told me a columnist from the *Philadelphia Bulletin* wanted to do a story about the prodigal novelist's triumphant return.

Meeting with Jim Smart at the newspaper's offices, I spent ninety minutes baring my soul to his questions. Afterward I waited apprehensively for his write-up, as there's no way to know how a journalist will reflect what passes through his filter. In Smart's case, I had no need to worry. He wrote a fair-minded recap of me, my book, and Rittenhouse beatniks in 750 well-chosen words. Beyond the background and local stuff, he quoted me as saying, "The beatniks have no spokesman but Kerouac and his crowd who make them look happy. I want to show what neurotic messes they are. People in their thirties still wandering around in beards and sandals need professional help, and there's nothing on earth sadder than a 40-year-old beatnik."

The piece was a fine teaser for the book's American edition still to come and allowed me the last laugh on Center City Sonny and the other beats who'd given us the ho-hum treatment in the square. It also told old friends we hadn't seen in years we were back in town.

Two days later as we were moving into our own apartment on Walnut Street, there was a note at the Weingrads to call John Logue. John had worked with me making up civil service tests, had faithfully corresponded with us during our European years, and had even ordered six copies of the English hardcover *Century* to pass around as "lenders." John wanted to throw us a party Saturday night. It was to be a literary evening, so presumably everyone there would be literate, many having read his lending copies of the book.

"Sounds like fun," I said, accepting.

The Logues—John, wife Evelyn, and eight-year-old Eileen—lived in an upgraded south Philadelphia row house, and when we walked over from the bus stop Saturday night, the narrow street was crowded with parked cars. Inside, several dozen people in their thirties and forties—most of whom we didn't know—stood around a refreshment table. The moment we stepped through the door, an expectant hush fell over the room. It was clear Juneau and I were the hub of the evening's entertainment.

Grabbing drinks for courage, we tried to blend into the crowd, but they would have none of that. A short man with a black Vandyke beard grabbed me by the elbow and hissed into my ear, "So what do you have against the U.S. of A., anyway?"

Smiling against my natural inclination, I replied, "I must love this crazy country. Otherwise I wouldn't be here."

Over my shoulder I saw Juneau being encircled just as a tall, skinny man with a bulging Adam's apple stepped up, shook my hand, and asked, "Is it true what they say about beatniks?"

"Maybe," I said. "If you tell me what they say, I'll tell you if it's true."

"Oh, you know." He poked me slyly in the ribs. "All the free sex you hear about . . . "

"Oh, that. Look, if I confess something to you, will you promise to keep it to yourself?"

"What is it? Yes!"

"Free sex is a misnomer," I whispered. "Everybody pays one way or the other."

"Oh, come on!" he said.

I was grateful when John came for us, led us to a pair of stuffed chairs in the middle of a ring of folding chairs, and sat us down.

"Might as well get down to it," he announced.

The guests settled quickly into their places, and the bearded man broached the real business of the evening.

"I read your book," he began, allowing a pregnant silence to build.

"You read John's lending library copies," I said to fill the gap. "That was the British version that came out a few months ago. The printer made us delete some parts before he would set type. But when the American edition comes out, it'll be the real truth, the whole truth, and nothing but the truth."

The beard frowned. "Actually, I don't expect a few minor additions or changes will affect your book radically," he said. "In my view, what you've written is very derivative, not very new, and has been done better by others. So my real question to you is, why did you feel compelled to write it?"

I felt my cheeks and neck heating up. After establishing the beard's name and calling—Stanford Strauss, psychology prof at Temple University—I challenged him to specify the authors he accused me of plagiarizing. He named Henry Miller and Jack Kerouac, and I quickly demolished his charge.

"How about all the phony experimentation?" piped in a skinny lady with Betty Boop auburn hair. "It's all so childish!"

As I tried to defend my creative use of type, others berated me for my "hatred of psychologists," "fear of homosexuality," and "contempt for intellectuals." I soon felt as if backed against a wall by junkyard dogs baying in my face. As I started rising from my chair, Juneau pushed me back down.

"Who are you people, anyway?" she shouted. "Which of you has ever published a book? Or even written one, for that matter! You bunch of critics! I don't respect a thing you say because none of you have paid any dues to criticize. Go put your own heads on the chopping block, set down your sweat and blood on paper, go halfway around the world to publish it and see how you feel about a bunch of do-nothings taking cheap shots at your work!"

John came over to console us. "I didn't plan this," he said. "You know how much I like the book."

"I know that, John," I said. "But it's no fun sitting here smiling like an idiot while your friends chew up me and my book. I'm hustling to find a job now, and I need every bit of ego I can hang on to. Let them bite chunks out of each other's hide, if that makes them happy. But we're splitting."

"I understand," John said.

That week I signed up as a substitute teacher in the Philadelphia public schools. Calling the school board each morning before seven, I was told if and where I was needed. When assigned, I'd gulp down corn flakes and coffee, jump on a bus, and try to arrive at my assigned school by 8:15—all for twenty dollars a day. I covered English and social studies classes at junior and senior high schools—almost all in the inner city, mostly poor black and minority students—where my role was mainly holding chaos at bay and keeping gang wars from breaking out at the blackboard.

Since Juneau was still not well enough to hold a job, every dollar counted. With job interviews intervening, I averaged about three teaching days a week—earning enough to pay the rent and put food on the table but leaving no margin for fun or error. Late one afternoon as I came home from a particularly trying stint with teenage brats, Juneau handed me a letter marked *Marquis Who's Who*. The form letter inside congratulated me on the unique talents that prompted the editorial board to add my biography "to those other 70,000 prominent Americans whose achievements have shaped the nation." Looking carefully for hidden price tags and finding none, I smartly filled in the form and mailed it back before they could change their minds.

The next week I got a call from a secretary at Chilton Publishing, setting up an interview for a research associate position. Chilton was another Main Line company located in the ritzy suburbs of Philly so, having been burned once by Smith Kline and French, I showed up that next Monday with no great hope in my heart. This time, though, everyone seemed most cordial, even friendly. Assistant research director Lyons Howland asked if I would take an aptitude test, and that Saturday I sat through three hours of IQ skullduggery at Drexel Institute of Technology.

A few days later, Chilton called me back and told me the test results were in, looked good, and could I come in to "discuss arrangements?" That afternoon I sat in Howland's office, relieved to have the fencing over with. He spelled out the hours and starting pay. I got him to up his salary offer a bit.

and we shook hands as new colleagues. The long depressing job of looking for work was over.

With my book's publication pushed back to January, the job kept my nerves steadied while I earned decent money for a change, allowing us the luxury of eating out, taking in movies, concerts, and jazz clubs, and blowing a few dollars on occasional idiocies. One evening, after playing tennis with John Logue and some other men friends, Dan Lerner of the clothing chain family made such wild claims for the uncanny powers of a local psychic we all decided to ante up five dollars each and put Madame Olga to the test.

When we got to her storefront address on South Street, the place was all dark except for a dim light filtered from a rear room. Undaunted, Dan rang the bell insistently until a light came on and Olga herself opened the door. Bleach blonde and fifty, her features matched the hardness of her glinty blue eyes.

"Yass? Vatt iss it you vant?" she asked.

"Just a reading," Dan said.

"We've heard so much about you," John said.

"It's too late. I'm closed." She started to close the door.

"But we all want readings," Dan said. "All six of us."

"Six?" The door opened again. "You must pay thirty dollars, then?"

"Right," John said.

She smiled for the first time. "Come in, gentlemen, and I vill giff you a special reading."

Latching the door behind us, she led us through a slit curtain into a dimly lit back room holding a slightly raised platform with a white backdrop. We took seats on folding chairs while Olga moved behind a podium holding a softball-sized crystal. Her eyes rolled back as she stared into the glass.

"Could you see if . . ." John began.

"Sssssshhhhhh," Olga commanded. "No talking, please!"

Waiting in the dull light promoted a spooky feeling, until I felt a prickly sensation at the back of my neck. The silence built until at last Olga opened her eyes and smiled professionally.

"I see some von here vith children," she said. "A schoolteacher—no, he vorks vith upset children—a psychiatrist." Jerry was a juvenile psychologist and a consultant to the Philadelphia school system. "Yess, you haff had difficult time this year. Your vife iss not vith you." A divorce was pending after a long separation. "Yess, next year you vill haff good times . . . new voman . . . and you get promotion, more money."

Jerry beamed at the good tidings as Olga's eyes closed again. More silence, then she said, "There iss one here who iss vatching over vurrkers . . ." An even bigger smile for John the time/motion man, but John kept his grim look frozen as he stared at Olga. "I see you changing job . . . more money, big company . . ." Still John did not crack. "One day, long time—is there Jan here? John?"

John was not going to identify himself until Lerner said, "This is John here!"

"Good," Olga grinned. "Some day, long time from now, you vill be very important man. A political man, mayor, something big, you see!"

John never even grinned, but the others slapped his back. Dan cracked, "Hey, why not go for president?" as Olga went back to work. This time a sour frown came on her face as she opened her eyes, and we hushed, expecting some dire prophecy.

"I see books, many books around you. Oceans, I see oceans . . . you travel much, very far . . ." The frown turned into an absolute grimace, as though seeing some disgusting object. "This one he writes the books . . . famous, many people around and he speaks to crowds—philosophy, religious things . . ."

The distaste on her face was so marked I found it hard to look at her, even though I knew she was talking about me. Finally, she shook her head and closed her eyes again.

"I see office . . . pictures, " Olga said, smiling again. "A man alone with many people, but so lonely he iss . . ."

On the drive home, we discussed her disjointed comments, scoring her for accuracy and agreeing it was remarkable how she called John by name.

"She probably heard one of you use it," John said. "You know she didn't see it in that glass ball of hers."

"Come on, John," I said. "Just believe and you'll be mayor."

"Sure," he said. "And you'll be Soren Kierkegaard. That's the easiest thirty bucks she'll ever see."

"Did you see the sour face she gave you?" Dan asked me.

"I was ready to ask for my money back. Good thing she said nice things."

"Notice," John said. "Everyone ended up a winner, nobody dies young, gets cancer, or goes bankrupt."

"Just goes to show what a superior bunch we are," I said.

As if to prove my boast, the next morning's mail brought a copy of a biographical print-out from Marquis identifying me as a "Writer/Author," along with a letter saying my entry would appear in the next issue of Who's Who in the East. The fact that I'd never published anything beyond a few poems in this country made me believe their intelligence network had overseas reach. At thirty-one, I felt it was proof positive I was "making it," and my head swelled along with my expectations. None of my contemporaries had made the book, nor had anyone in my immediate family—though a distant cousin who painted and lived in France was in Who's Who in the World, a goal I considered worthy of future attainment.

I basked in the Marquis glow and used my spare time to scheme up ways to promote my book's upcoming publication, now set for February. Yoseloff wrote that advance sales had hit fifteen hundred, "excellent for a first novel that demands so much from its readers."

The New Year started full of promise with book publication just a month away, but a phone call from Thomas Yoseloff threw a monkey wrench into our plans. He was extending the publication date to May to give his publicity and marketing people more time to "do it justice."

At work, Ed Richter, former newspaperman and now a staff writer for Chilton magazines, cozied up to me, using coffee breaks and overdesk exchanges for book world chat. The year before, Richter had published *They Pay Me to Catch Footballs,* a book on Philadelphia Eagles wide receiver Tommy McDonald, and he had just come out with *The Making of a Big-League Pitcher,* a virtual textbook for would-be hurlers. Learning of my passion for sports, he'd given me a copy of his baseball book, inscribing the flyleaf "For Dave Chagall, with best wishes—Rom. 8:28." So ignorant was I of things biblical, I thought it referred to a room number or a date. As things turned out, "8:28" would prove prophetic in more ways than one.

May arrived, and my book came out. Where in England it was reviewed everywhere, if with mixed enthusiasm, here it ran into a stone wall of silence. Aside from one mildly encouraging paragraph in *Library Journal*—"a first novel for those who can afford to support the promising"—the American literary establishment reacted mostly by ignoring it and hoping it would go away. The *Chicago Sun-Times* was the only big-city paper to take note, conceding that "Chagall's stream-of-consciousness style is fine and the narrative free-flowing and probing—but it's all been said too much, too often." In the weeks following publication, friends kept asking me when the book was coming out, and I had the embarrassing task of explaining it already was. Even the *Evening Bulletin,* whose slogan boasted it was read by every Philadelphian, refused to print a Yoseloff ad scheduled for late May. When I went to see the paper's advertising manager to ask why, he said the ad was rejected on the advice of the Better Business Bureau because it referred to the "denizens of Philadelphia's bohemian sector near fashionable Rittenhouse Square," which the BBB felt would be bad for business. Already enraged by the reviewing blackout, I raised First Amendment threats, which seemed to totally underwhelm the adman. So I called on the ACLU's Spencer Coxe who promised to remind the *Bulletin* of its constitutional obligations. Two days later the adman called me at work, his voice and manner suitably subdued, to say his paper would be happy to run the ad as is.

Early in June the first ad ran, and friends stopped asking when my book was coming out. However, when they went to department stores to buy it, the clerks took it out from its hiding place under the counter since it was considered "controversial." Despite the book's being such a well-kept secret, it sold out a second printing and became the rebels' bible at UC-Berkeley, inspiring the *Barb, L.A. Free Press,* and other alternate papers to adopt my printing innovations as standard style for the underground press.

As they might have said in Sweden, I was "world famous in Beatsville."

7

Civil Rights and Wrongs

L ife soon rushed in to crowd out the disappointing reception for my book. After suffering severe abdominal cramps, Juneau visited a prominent gynecologist who diagnosed a possibly cancerous tumor he insisted must come out at once. So in mid-June I found myself once more in a hospital waiting room, praying to Whomever It Concerned for the life of my wife under a surgeon's knife. This time happily proved less hazardous. After a few hours Dr. Feldman came out in his pale green smock to say how well things had gone. The fibroid tumor he'd removed was benign; Juneau was healthy and therefore should heal quickly. In fact, she spent the next three months recuperating from the ordeal.

One afternoon while I was at work, Juneau had a surprise visit from Wendy DeLeo. She told an incredible tale of what really happened to her husband. Al had become more and more involved with Theosophy and, after shaving his head, he regarded himself as a called-out monk who needed to devote all his waking hours to metaphysics. After a few months of unemployment and Theosophical studies, he'd left her and returned to his hometown, Los Angeles. Wendy visited him there and met his family in East L.A. His real name was Delgado, not DeLeo, and he was Mexican, not Italian. Absorbing that shock, she arranged to go back to

Philadelphia and live with her parents while he got established. Then, he assured her, he'd send for her and the kids.

A few months later, his mother called to break the bad news. Al had borrowed money from a street banker to open a restaurant and couldn't pay it back on time. When three of the shylock's musclemen shoved him into a car and drove out to the canyons, Al was sure they meant to waste him and dump his body into the brush. So he pulled his own gun, killed the driver and wounded another man. The two surviving thugs beat him mercilessly and left him for dead at the side of the road. The police found him and took him to the hospital. He was later convicted of murder and sentenced to forty years in San Quentin.

Wendy's mother tended the kids now while she was back at school, working toward a teaching degree. Her final divorce papers were due in a few weeks, and even she found it hard to believe her own story. It appeared Blavatsky's "insights" did Al little good.

Summer living seemed easy with a light schedule at work, weeknight parties with the Logues, and weekend fishing trips to Cape May with Ron Weingrad. A new spurt of writing energy enlivened me, and I found myself back at short stories, a form I hadn't tried in years. But just as we were relaxing into the "good life," trouble popped up to make sure we didn't get too comfortable. One afternoon Juneau returned from a follow-up visit to Dr. Feldman, looking harried.

"What's wrong?" I asked.

She shook her head. "Nothing. Why do you ask?"

"Come on," I said. "What did Feldman say?"

"He said I've healed fine, everything's fine—really."

"You sure?"

"Certainly." She forced a grin, and I dropped it.

Over the next few days Juneau went about her chores in a dark mood. Over dinner one night she finally owned up to what was troubling her. During her last visit to the gynecologist's office, the doctor violated her helpless examination position by molesting her. Then when she fought her way off the table, he tried to embrace her. My first instinct was to go punch his face in. When I grew more calm, I suggested the man had to be reported. Juneau feared that "snitching" might provoke retaliation, but after talking it over, she agreed we had to stop him from doing it to others.

The next morning I called the County Medical Society. When I told the director what happened, he began arguing with me, suggesting that women are "overly sensitive" and often imagine sexual advances that never occur. That set me off. I threatened to call the papers or turn it over to a lawyer, and he grew more conciliatory.

"Write a letter to my attention," he said. "Describe exactly what took place, and I promise you the Board of Censors will quickly deal with the situation."

That afternoon I mailed a letter detailing the unsavory details and urging the society to take whatever steps necessary to ensure that no other woman suffer such indignities. I also sent a note to Dr. Feldman, informing him I'd reported his swinish behavior to the society.

A short reply from the Medical Society arrived a few days later, assuring us the complaint would soon be acted on. Ten days later I wrote again to learn the Board of Censors did not meet during summer months—"Your complaint will be considered at its next meeting September 19." Though the wheel of justice turned too slowly, at least it did grind along—or so I thought.

One morning at work Ed Richter asked to lunch together, and as we walked to a little Chinese place nearby, we talked books. Over wonton soup, in his quiet, unassuming manner, Ed asked how I felt about black people. Since one of my closest work buddies was a long, lean Kenyan named Martin Mutisya, I thought it would be obvious and said so.

"Sure, but it's one thing getting along with the son of a Nairobi minister," Ed pointed out. "It could be tougher relating to a sharecropper's kid."

"I see your point," I said. "But other than not being colorblind, I figure black people deserve the same chance at pursuing happiness as any other American. The Constitution guarantees it, even if some bigots disagree. Just look around Chilton, and you'll see how far we have to go."

"I have," Ed said. "We each do what we can. How'd you like to go light a candle for civil rights?"

"How?"

"Join a group of us next Wednesday going to Washington, D.C."

"Sounds like fun. Where do we meet and what time?"

He handed me a flyer promoting a march on Washington, then we settled in to enjoy our pork fried rice and discuss the great year Sandy Koufax was having for the Dodgers.

That next Wednesday was August 28—the same 8:28 he'd inscribed in his book, though (I was to find out much later) its least important significance. At 5:15 on that particular morning, when most sane people roll over to their left side for another hour of sleep, I found myself outside the Seventh Presbyterian Church in north Philadelphia amid a sea of black and white faces. I couldn't find Ed, so I went inside and slipped into a seat at the rear of the sanctuary. Looking over the crowd buzzing with conversation, I was disappointed to find the talk segregated, black with black and white with white.

"Please, everyone, kindly be seated!" shouted a fortyish black man in a pinstripe suit and rep tie.

The seats quickly filled, and everyone stared expectantly at the pulpit, which was soon occupied by a chunky black man in shirt sleeves. The man smiled warmly.

"This is supposed to be a briefing, and I'm supposed to give it," he said. "So please bear with me. My name is Terrance Roberts, and I'm minister of Fourth Presbyterian on Oxford Street. First, let's be clear about the purposes of this march. What it *isn't* is more clear, perhaps, than what it is. It is *not* a sit-in, drive-in, or passive resistance thing. What we want to do is impress the people in Washington with the extent of our commitment to the cause of civil rights—and to do this without, I repeat, *without* incident."

The Reverend Roberts paused to let it sink in before going on.

"Now there are folks going down there for the sole purpose of causing trouble. They include contingents from the

American Nazi party and the Muslims. Whatever they may do or say, *please, please* refrain from reacting. You old ball-players here, we know you can beat up on any Nazi or Muslim ever born—please don't try to prove it. When we arrive in Washington, we'll be told where to go and how to get there. That means you got to stay together with our great group here or you're likely to get lost in the shuffle. They say there may be more than a hundred thousand people there, and that's an awful lot of folks to look for a hundred of our own. Any questions?"

Mumbles from the crowd, but no one spoke.

"Okay, then." Roberts glanced at his watch. "The bus leaves in exactly thirty-seven minutes. Coffee and donuts are in the vestibule. Remember to stay together, and may the Lord bless this day!"

The crowd responded with amens, yeahs, and hallelujahs like the rally before the big game. As everyone stood and re-formed into small clusters, I spotted Ed coming through the front door and waved, but he headed for Rev. Roberts without acknowledging he saw me. They chatted animatedly a few minutes, and when Roberts broke away, I went over to him.

"Five o'clock you said?" I needled.

"Oh, there you are—what time did you get here?"

"Twenty minutes before you."

"I was tied up at home, the kids, domesticity, all the rest of it." Ed smiled winningly. "How 'bout coffee?"

Competition at the food tables was fierce. I was inclined to hang back and wait, but Ed pushed ahead, dragging me with him. Taking a rough check, I counted a three-to-one ratio, blacks over whites. Good thing we were on the same team. Asking myself *why* for the tenth time since I agreed to come, I came up with the same semivalid answers. First, the march seemed a good way to strike a blow for justice. Then there was my writer's curiosity, ever looking for a new experience, and to be where the action was. Finally, as a Jew I felt the black struggle was somehow my own battle. During childhood gang fights against the German kids from Sixth Street, they always taunted us that a Jew was nothing more than a black turned inside out. Deep inside, I must have agreed with them.

Grabbing a cup of coffee, I turned to say something to Ed—he was gone again. Spotting him twenty feet away talking to a man with a mustache, I lit a cigarette and walked over, waiting a few minutes before he noticed me.

"Harry, this is Dave Chagall. He works with me," Ed said.

"Good to meet you," Harry said shaking hands. "Are you Jewish . . . or . . ."

"Jewish," I said.

"Not that it matters," he said. "Just a little surprising for the Presbyterian Interracial Council . . . heh, heh."

"It's cheaper riding down with you," I said, and from the frown pulling down Harry's lips I knew my usual sense of tact had hit home.

"Harry Carsons is my pastor," Ed said. "Second Presbyterian of Mayfair, a heck of a guy."

"I'll take your word on it," I said.

Harry spotted another member of his flock and hurried off to tend her.

"Dave, you're too hard on people," Ed said.

"Part of my charm," I said.

"You've got Carsons wrong. He doesn't give a darn whether you're Moslem, Jewish, or atheist. You're oversensitive. You know that, don't you?"

"Just a hangover from my kid days when I had troubles with Lutherans who looked like a gang of young Carsons."

Spotting another familiar face, Ed took off. This time I felt more at ease on my own, and I smoked and drank my coffee in peace. Fifteen minutes later the call came to board the bus. I could feel the excitement start to build.

The ride south was mostly anticipation and small talk. Ed rode on the outside of our double-seat, interspersing civil rights talk with abrupt dashes to familiar faces and back again for further declamations on race equality and rotten injustices of the status quo. Frankly, I was disappointed by the screamingly middle-class faces around me, the blacks more square than the white—if that were possible. I would have felt infinitely more comfortable with a carload of beatniks, where at least there would have been some passion and real racial closeness. Time dragged by. I never knew what hit me when I fell asleep.

I awakened to a subtle stir, an imperceptible quickening of breathing and feet scraping against rubber matting. Out the window, we saw small detached houses flow by, then a lone filling station and a dusty diner as we passed through the outskirts until we reached the tightly packed row houses of the nation's capital. Block after block the lawns were filled with black folks—kids, old women, men in shirt sleeves—all waving and cheering as we rode by with our red-and-white Presbyterian Interracial Council banner proclaiming our loyalties.

For the first time all morning, emotions began to stir. Tears filled my eyes, and understanding filtered into my heart as to why I had come. The welcoming locals reminded me of films I'd seen of American GIs in World War II as they thrust through villages and towns on their way to liberating Paris. Their naive trust humbled my spirit as I realized how they saw this march on Washington—in their eyes we were an army of Americans dedicated to the liberation of black people throughout the land, brave as the revolutionaries of old. I felt shamed, knowing my motives were unworthy of their faith.

When the bus parked at the curbside of the staging area, we made our way to the Washington Monument area where we endured a series of cheerleading speeches over portable loudspeakers. When the word finally came down to form ranks, cheers of relief rang out. Monitors with green armbands passed out placards, banners, and March On Washington buttons, then we lined up four abreast and waited for the signal to head down Independence and Constitution avenues toward the Lincoln Memorial. Finally, the ranks ahead moved out—the march was on.

Federal workers on their lunch hour lined the sidewalks and watched curiously as we passed. An occasional camera came out to click shots of the marchers as we stepped along, singing songs about freedom.

I found myself listening hard to the words and tunes until I hesitantly joined in and then let myself bellow heartily with the rest. Looking around, I saw that Anglo reserve limited many white faces to apologetic mouthing of words. Some grinned self-consciously but did not sing, while union contingents carried their LGWU and AFL-CIO MANHATTAN banners with stoic boredom. As we came up to one intersection, a network boom stretching across the middle of the street pointed a television camera at the parade, its relentless red eye glowing "On Air." As the marchers passed by, banners waved more vigorously, and the singing grew boisterous.

"Hold those signs higher!" Rev. Carsons urged the standard bearers for the Presbyterian Interracial Council.

And our arms stretched heavenward while we sang, "Marching on to freedom, we will not be moved!"

Snaking along the streets, we finally reached the grassy plots fronting the Memorial where discipline suddenly broke. I was awestruck by what was undoubtedly the largest crush of humanity I'd ever seen. Turning to Ed, I said, "Really impressive . . ."

But Ed was gone. And so were the rest of the Presbyterian Interracial Council. By now the event had come to resemble a gigantic family picnic. Blankets had appeared all over the great grassy expanse, and small groups sat sharing food and drinks. Young people flirted while others listened to speeches blaring out loudspeakers mounted on poles or more intimately through transistor radios. Folk singers folksang, film stars promoted themselves using a civil rights backdrop, and black authors—Jimmy Baldwin among them—raised the level of outrage with impassioned, inflammatory rhetoric that somehow managed to be dull and predictable. Still, no one left with the sun at three o'clock and sinking.

Just as folks started to doze off, a platoon of Nazis—ablaze with swastikas and swagger—marched on to the Memorial grounds behind Commandant Lincoln Rockwell. Sitting in a circle, arms crossed across their chests, they began shouting inflammatory racial insults. Deep-throated grumbles in the crowd turned into angry growls when a phalanx of NAACP marshals quickly surrounded the Brown Shirts. Grim-faced, they stood there in a menacing circle, provoking a waiting silence from the onlookers until a squad of uniformed police moved in to escort the Nazis out of the area.

The Muslims, some wearing red fezzes, circulated through the crowd but—aside from their quaint garb—they excited little reaction. The lack of confrontation was a big letdown, particularly after all the media hype warning of thuggery and race riots. Fear kept lots of timid liberals home, but it soon grew clear the day would produce no martyrs. Eventually, the mood grew sleepy, even apathetic. People stretched out on blankets, dozed, and baked in the sun. Even Roy Wilkins who spoke passionately, intelligently, and full of truth prompted just polite applause. What more could anyone say, preaching to a choir who long ago had accepted the notion of equal rights as ridiculously self-evident?

Wandering around, I found Ed with Rev. Carsons seated on a retaining wall a quarter-mile from the speakers' platform, talking baseball, trade unions, and the affluent society. As yet another speaker was introduced, Carsons glanced at his watch.

"Three-thirty," he said. "Another hour and a half should wind it up."

"The important thing is at least we've done something, taken some sort of action," Ed said. "That's a whole lot better than sitting around the church moaning over the plight of black people."

"Exactly my sentiments," Carsons said. "Too many of us are happy to pay lip service for equality but unwilling to put any force behind our words. At least we're here . . ."

". . . chained on slave ships from Africa!" bellowed a voice from the loudspeakers.

Shadows lengthened, bringing a chill to the air. I slipped on my suit jacket, ate a banana, and half-listened to the words cutting through the late afternoon stupor.

"I still have a dream. It is a dream deeply rooted in the American Dream. I have a dream that one day this nation will rise up and live out the true meaning of its creed. We hold these truths to be self-evident, that all men are created equal."

Something about that voice was remarkably different, it vibrated with a passion and energy that made us shut up and listen. Every word seemed hypnotically important, bursting with meaning, full of power.

Resonant the voice, reverent its intonations. Everyone was listening, a mighty gathering of half a million souls united and spellbound as one. Captured by an extraordinary moment in time, we thrilled to the spirit-filled tones that swelled through the electronics, washing in warm waves over the grassy expanse, each word hanging clear and meaningful so all could marvel. Our collective breath caught as he paused, our hearts skipped a beat—until with a rush we were swept back with the amplified oratory that seemed to be framed like skywriting across the firmament.

". . . when we let freedom ring, when we let it ring from every village and every hamlet, from every state and every city, we will be able to speed up that day when all of God's children, black men and white men, Jews and gentiles, Protestants and Catholics, will be able to join hands and sing in the words of that old Negro spiritual—'Free at last, free at last! Thank God almighty, we are free at last!'"

When the voice fell silent, the hush was pierced by one sudden cry that grew to a mighty roar as cheers rushed in to rent the heavens with huzzahs, amens, hallelujahs, and God bless you's! I found myself yelling past the clog in my throat, happy tears flowing down my cheeks. Beside me, Ed was clapping like mad and Carsons grinned with real appreciation. A full four minutes the ovation roared like a waterfall until at last it softened, diminished, and faded into small pockets of cheering that gave way to a marveling buzz.

The program moved on. Marian Anderson sang, other speakers followed, but echoes of that lone voice overshadowed anything mere fleshly talent could produce. The day ended with an invocation. People gathered their belongings and drifted toward where the chartered buses were parked.

Talk turned to weather, family, and work. But the good feeling followed along like a bright cloud as the marchers split for their separate if unequal long rides home, knowing they'd been witnesses at the making of history.

◆

After September 19 came and went without hearing from the Medical Society, I called them. A Dr. Weiner told me the Censor Board had considered our complaint against Dr. Feldman and would act on it. He named 4:30 on the afternoon of October 17 for Juneau to appear before the board and testify.

The society was headquartered in a paneled brownstone on South Twenty-First Street. Inside, amid the smell of pomposity and high fees, an unfriendly receptionist kept Juneau and me waiting on hard wooden benches for twenty minutes before another unsmiling staffer came for us and escorted us into the hearing room where six physicians sat on one side of a long conference table.

We sat across from them on low chairs, and a lead inquisitor started the questioning. Juneau recalls the ordeal . . .

Eyes focused on me from across the table. I felt embarrassed as I was asked to describe in detail what had happened to me during a post-operative examination. I spoke carefully, trying to use clinical words to report the incident. As I spoke, I could read the skepticism in their faces. The medical clique was protecting its own. Men protect other men, while society condemns women, *I thought.*

They wanted to know why Dr. Feldman had acted the way he did. How could I answer why? That was my *question, too. Why, indeed? I didn't tell them about my feelings—the shock I still carried from the episode, the helplessness, shame, and broken trust. Because of my weakened state just after*

*the surgery, I was totally vulnerable, depending on
my doctor to heal me. That was why my fears had
been so magnified. I felt angry, but still too weak to
fight the medical system. Curiously, I was afraid
I'd hinder the progress of my healing if I changed
doctors so soon after the operation.*

*After the assault, I held off going to a doctor for
nearly two months, afraid of a recurrence. When I
finally did go to have my incision checked, I chose a
university hospital, arranging in advance to make
sure a nurse was present during the doctor's examination. Even so, it was awful.*

Finally, the ordeal ended. As we walked out, we passed
Dr. Feldman sitting on a chair waiting his turn. He would
not meet our eyes, and at least I had the satisfaction of seeing
shame in his hangdog expression—though I would have pre-
ferred rearranging his nose for him.

Follow-up calls to Dr. Weiner were not returned, and
the staffers there either did not know the board's decision or
were instructed to say they did not know. Finally in mid-
November, we received a letter from the society advising
"that the Board has acted upon the matter under discussion
at that time." It sounded good, but who knew what it meant?
I tried again to get somebody there to spell out their actions,
but hit the same stone wall of silence.

When a friend telephoned Feldman's office, she determined he was still in business, still booking appointments,
and still examining vulnerable women. Larry Littlejohn, a
neurosurgeon who'd given up his practice after a nervous
breakdown, told us the board had done little more than slap
Feldman's wrist with a professional rebuke. The medical fra-
ternity, he said, invariably protected its own.

"One thing, though," Larry added. "Now that Juneau's
testimony is part of their record, the next time someone reports him, they can be legally culpable along with Feldman.
So I'm sure they told him to shape up."

My birthday came around a few days later, but what

began as a personal celebration soon blew up in my face. Just before lunch, Brenda Block came rushing into the research room.

"Kennedy's been shot!" she said.

There was a stunned silence, then the questions erupted—Where? When? Who? Brenda had no answers, so we found a radio and listened to the spotty reports coming in from Dallas. For ninety minutes we reacted to the scanty updates, hoping against hope that the president would survive. He represented a new start for America, the kind of leadership we'd been waiting for and a big part of the changing national mood that brought us back from Europe. But now, we soon learned, the king was truly dead. Lyndon Johnson took over, and a new, ominous era was born.

Since nobody could even eat lunch, let alone do any useful work, Chilton management sent us all home. Juneau and I spent the afternoon in front of the TV set, listening to anchormen rehash late tidbits of news from Dallas, Washington, and the rest of the world.

Kennedy's murder left us devastated. It was the third strike following our crushed hopes over the book, then Juneau's surgery and abuse. This loss was the final straw. We'd lost heart with my hometown that had welcomed us with the ardor of a soppy dishrag. That weekend we did lots of late-night bedtalking, heart to heart and soul to soul. We decided to run once more—only this time not overseas. This time we'd take our hurts, hopes, dreams, and schemes to California where—we'd heard—it was always spring, opportunities abounded, and nothing was impossible.

When I gave notice at work, some seemed shocked, others were inconvenienced, and a few were saddened. The latter were the ones I would miss. That week I wrote a dozen research and publishing firms in Los Angeles, gave them a little background, and said I'd be in touch when we arrived.

We bought a VW Microbus for $950, outfitted it with foam mattresses, a camping stove, lantern, and flashlights, loaded it with all the furniture and clothes it would hold, and then gave away everything else. It was the first hippy wagon of the sixties, long before the word *hippy* had been coined, complete with tobacco pouch full of marijuana and seeds to sow in California.

On a chilly day in early December, while snowflakes fell and slush sloshed over center city streets, we traded tearful good-byes with the few friends who really cared, climbed in our VW, and headed for the Pennsylvania Turnpike.

8

The Last Frontier

Though sleet turned to driving rain as we neared Pittsburgh, our spirits were sustained by visions of eternal sunshine beckoning ahead. In one of the "Betty books," her spirit guide describes the afterlife as "Summerland," where the grass is always green and everyone is eternally, playfully young. Juneau had lived in Los Angeles as a child, returning briefly after college to act in little theater, so her vision of California dreamin' was based on more reality than mine.

We saw the West Coast as the end of the road, the place to make our last stand with the Pacific at our backs. A few friends had already made the trek. One was working as a cameraman for Columbia Pictures, another managed up-and-coming rock groups, and a third—who had married the sister of playwright Larry *A Funny Thing Happened on the Way to the Forum* Gelbart, was trying to break into TV writing.

But we had loads of road to travel before we got there. We gained a trueblue view of these United States driving the fully loaded, top-heavy, four-cylinder VW that couldn't roll faster than sixty-five miles per hour downhill and was far slower climbing grades in low gear. It gave us time to count farmhouses, smell the pine trees and listen to what was in people's hearts.

Our fourth night out, we ate a late supper in a shabby Amarillo cafe. It was after ten o'clock, and we were bone weary. Instead of moving on to look for a place to bed down, we decided to crash right there in the parking lot behind a saloon.

It took just a few minutes for us to lock the car doors, close the curtains, change into pajamas, and crawl into our bunk. Staring up at the VW's ceiling three inches above our faces, we fell fast asleep. An instant later, or so it seemed, we were roused by shouts and curses that sounded right on top of us. Wide-eyed, we listened to the thumps and grunts of a fistfight until our wagon jolted under the impact of a hurtling body.

"You—. I'm gonna kill you!" yelled a voice just outside. Then came the sounds of rushing boots, bellowing, more cursing, and a deep-throated faraway voice calling for the combatants to "knock it off!"

"—you, you—!" came the the reply.

The next sound was the sharp crack of a pistol or rifle shot that echoed and faded. The curses and shouting ceased. Someone whispered, another mumbled, then came the sound of shuffling feet moving away. We waited for more, but the show was over. My watch glowed 3:25.

"Welcome to Texas, you-all," I cracked.

We managed a few more hours of sleep before getting up to a new day. The gray predawn light gave the parking lot an innocent look. But with the dark memories of last night's strife still vividly on our minds, we quickly pulled on our street clothes and were back on the road again.

A few hours later, we ate heartily in Tucumcari, New Mexico, a name that rolled trippingly off the tongue. People were open and friendly, and we headed off to Albuquerque in an upbeat mood. We took time off to walk around the city, and we were so impressed we vowed to return as soon as we could.

As the late afternoon sun dipped low, a fierce chill gripped our bones. Since we hadn't brought along any tough cold-weather clothing, we stopped off at a thrift store and bought two heavily-lined jackets for five dollars each. After eating at a downtown Mexican restaurant, we parked near the zoo, pulled the jackets over our street garb, and hunkered into cozy blankets. Frost tweaked our noses as we spent the coldest night of our lives huddled together, teeth chattering and breath misting.

"Let's come back to Albuquerque," Juneau suggested. "In summertime."

Driving toward Gallup the following morning, the mountains began rising steeply and we had to shift down for most of the climb. It took us three hours to cross into Arizona but, after lunch, we made up the time on a downhill run to Holbrook. The air was still icy and so was the road, making driving high adventure. We decided to head for warmer climes and avoid the uphill mileage to Flagstaff by leaving Route 66. That would prove an almost fatal mistake. As we began a southward descent on a narrow byway marked AZ 77, the sights were awesome—steep canyons, rising pines, and that cloudless Arizona sky—but the narrow two-lane byway wound around like a corkscrew, putting extra strain on brakes, wheels, gears and driver. About a half-hour into the detour, the car started to vibrate, and only by slowing to a crawl could we get rid of the shaking. We thought we were in luck when we passed a sign reading Shumway 3 Miles. But when we reached town, we found a dozen houses surrounding a tiny country store—and no service station.

A wizened old man sat behind the counter reading a paper. Watching us over the top of his glasses as we entered, he put the paper down. When we told him about our car trouble, he advised us to head for Show Low "just a piece ahead." After a hair-raising ride over a winding ski slope of a road, we limped into town and pulled into its lone service station.

The mechanic quickly found out what was wrong, but he'd have to go to Globe, seventy miles away, to get the part we needed. Almost three hours to the minute after he left, the young man returned—empty handed.

"We're out of luck," he said cheerfully. "The parts place has to order a shaft collar from the distributor in Phoenix."

I moaned, envisioning a week's wait as our nest egg slowly evaporated.

Juneau groaned. "Can't you do anything to fix it without the collar?"

"Well," he said. "I could put a shim in there. That should fix it until you get to where you're going."

He wriggled under the car, and we listened to sounds of scraping and banging. Twenty minutes late he emerged, grinning.

"That ought to hold you," he said.

Relief was written all over the smiles on our faces. "Thanks a lot. What's your name, anyway?"

"Randy," he said. "Randy Wilson. I like your car. You got it fixed up real cool. Come all the way from Pennsylvania, have you?"

We talked awhile, and when he discovered our passion for the arts, he took us to a back room where he kept examples of his handiwork—carved totem poles with the faces of blacks, Indians, and Anglo Westerners interspersed. The workmanship was elaborate, the wood sanded and finished into a marbleized texture that highlighted the grain.

After admiring his work, we prepared to leave.

"How much do we owe you?" I asked.

"Nothing," Randy said.

"We have to pay you for your work," Juneau said. "You earned it."

"No, please," he said. And he adamantly refused to accept payment. "Just remember me when you get to L.A.," Randy called as we pulled out.

It was already dark as we headed for Phoenix. The car rode smoother than it had before the breakdown, and in a world where kindness seemed lost forever, we knew we'd remember Randy and Show Low long after we reached Los Angeles. Like forever, maybe.

The rest of the trip was trouble-free if a grind. Weary, bleary-eyed, and sick of driving, we finally reached L.A. and drove down the Sunset Strip looking for the apartment building where Rittenhouse Square refugee Ed Tickner lived. It was dinnertime, and colorful characters roamed the street. When we found his place, we rang the bell, but there was no answer. Waiting for Tickner to show, we fell asleep in the front seat of the VW.

Next morning at 6:30, we went for breakfast and found the streets empty. After eating at a nearby cafe and sightseeing to kill time, at 9:00 we returned to the apartments and rang Tickner's bell again. Again no answer. Three more tries, and we were about to leave when the door creaked open on a chain.

"Who's there?" croaked a graveyard voice.

It was Ed Tickner, still in his pajamas and obviously not quite awake. Once our identities penetrated his fog, a broad smile and wide open door welcomed us in. While he shaved and dressed, we filled him in on happenings back East. Then over instant coffee, he told us of the transformations Hollywood had wrought on his life.

With a business degree from the University of Miami, Florida, Ed had worked as an accountant for the federal government in Washington, DC. Hoping to do the same with a big film studio for lots more money, he'd come to Los Angeles—and instead got a job keeping books for rock impresario Al Grossman. Not content to work for a salary, Ed launched a side business managing actors and rock musicians, which had flourished so well that now, he believed, he was about to hit pay dirt with two groups—The Allman Brothers and The Byrds. His eyes glowed so brightly with prospects of success we acted impressed even if not wholly convinced.

We piled in his Oldsmobile, and he gave us a whirlwind tour of the area—Beverly Hills, Santa Monica, Topanga Canyon, Venice, and back to the Sunset Strip. Then Ed had to leave to check out his clients, some of them already notorious for drug freakouts, rioting and other unsocial acts.

The moment he left, we searched the L.A. Times for rentals, circled a few lower priced likelies and, armed with a street map, went looking for a new home. It was still early afternoon. Most of the good values seemed to be in Topanga

Canyon, which had impressed us with its wild and woolly charm. We found the realtor named in the ads after a long climb in low gear.

She wasted no time getting to the point. "How much can you pay?"

"Your ad said $150," I said.

"Yes, but that's quite rustic."

"We like it rustic," Juneau said.

"Fine, here's the address," the realtor said. "You'll find a shower outside the house, and there's a root cellar behind the back porch. If you like it, we can close the lease today."

She gave us a key, a map, and the address. Sitting in the parking lot, we finally found our street, traced our route on the roughly sketched contours, and pulled out. The way led up, and the road grew more narrow, rutted, and steep. Our four cylinders chugged hard to make the grade, while the climb angle soon seemed to reach 45° as we reached the next to last approach street. Making a left onto the mountain peak, the car engine coughed and stalled.

We got out to check the situation. It was even worse than we thought. Our front wheels were just inches from the right road shoulder, which plunged straight down into California's answer to the Grand Canyon. The other bank was only five feet away, leaving no room for error.

With Juneau standing outside to direct, I revved up the motor, tried juking back and forth, but when that raised a scream from Juneau, I backed it down the way we'd come, inch by inch, sweating blood for twenty minutes until I reached the cross street where I could back it around front first.

The moment I got it straightened out, Juneau struggled in on legs shaking from fear and gave me a big hug.

"I was really scared," she said. "I was sure both you and the car were hurtling down the canyon."

"That made two of us," I admitted.

When we got back to the realtor's office, she was gone, so we left her the keys and a note wishing the future tenant all the luck they would need.

The next day, bright, sunny, and hot, was Christmas.

Since we couldn't go house hunting, Ed suggested recharging our batteries down at Muscle Beach in Santa Monica. The sand was crawling with baking oily bodies, sucking up the golden rays. Watching the body builders flex their biceps amused us for a few minutes. Then plunking down on our towels, we soon succumbed to the afternoon heat and fell into the twilight zone of sun worship. Suddenly, the incongruity hit us.

"Do you realize this is Christmas?" Juneau said. "It seems so strange being on the beach Christmas Day."

"Enjoy it," Tickner said. "Last Christmas it rained like mad. Today's a special case."

The people around us looked like any beach crowd you might find in Atlantic City, except that more of them were fair-skinned blonds. Some teenagers were playing boxball on the hard sand along the water's edge, a few collegiate types tossed a football, and a handful of hardy souls actually swam in the swelling surf. That was when the thought hit me—how does anybody get any work done?

Saturday night, Tickner invited us to a concert at Santa Monica Civic where The Byrds were opening for a hot young songwriter-singer named Bob Dylan. The auditorium was jammed with screaming, swooning teenagers ready to roar at the slightest provocation. Taped rock pounded from the revved-up speakers, and the acrid smell of marijuana was so thick you could get buzzed just taking a deep breath.

We looked all over for Tickner but couldn't find him, so we stood in a side aisle and waited. Finally, The Byrds came on, electronically amplified, guitar-twanging gyrators performing their own original tunes, which somehow all managed to sound the same. Occasionally, youngsters who'd memorized their records would sing along so we could make out a few phrases, but the meaning and themes of their songs eluded us.

But if we found The Byrds obscure, at least they seemed to sing on key with recognizable harmonies. Bob Dylan was introduced with a reverence normally reserved for a pope or president. Dylan, a short, unimpressive-looking man wearing a blue work shirt and jeans, came out with a harmonica wired to his mouth. Holding a guitar stiffly in his left hand, he had a strained look on his face.

He seemed painfully shy as he cradled the guitar in his right arm, plucked a few warm-up chords, and then held still waiting for the right moment. The crowd hush grew so intense a few weaker vessels could not bear the tension, loosing painful screams. His fingers fluttered; he mumbled something into the mike by way of introduction and launched into his number. After listening for several minutes while the teenyboppers moaned ecstatically, Juneau looked at me quizzically, and I shook my head in sad agreement. Beyond doubt, this was one of the worst singing acts we'd ever heard.

Consistently out of key, Dylan screeched all the high notes and garbled his words. We managed to bear it for two full numbers, but during the third, we reached our limit. Hoping Tickner would not spot us, we slunk up the aisle, fought our way past the standing-room crowd, and plunged out the doors, gulping in the good fresh ocean air when we hit the street. Over breakfast the next day, Tickner asked how we liked the concert.

"Really interesting," I said. "Amazing the variety of sounds they get out of those amplified guitars."

Happily, Ed took it as affirmation and beamed his approval. He'd made new converts to the gospel of rock-and-roll.

That next week we rented a cottage in a Santa Monica apartment court, just off Wilshire Boulevard. Reasonably close to UCLA and the San Diego freeway, it was owned by a Dane named Jepsen who occupied the front unit. After living for weeks in our Microbus, the two-room facility with kitchen, bath, and adjoining garage seemed like a castle.

I called the research companies I'd written to and went to see two that expressed interest. Both said they had no real need for new people but should anything pop up, they'd be in touch. Taking it for a polite "no thanks," I turned to the *Times* classifieds, churned out a batch of resumes, and mailed them out. Meanwhile, spotting a temporary opening for men with cars to deliver telephone directories, I called, and the two of us drove to the telephone company where we were hired on the spot as piece workers. We spent the rest of the afternoon hauling stacks of phone books across Santa Monica for about two dollars an hour each.

When we'd worked that city dry, they sent us out to nearby Brentwood and kept us busy for two weeks until the job was done. After the heady corporate stuff I'd just left, the low prestige work was a fine antidote to any fake pride we'd developed. As if to reward us, the next week I got a call from Arne Haug—West Coast branch of the Roper Organization—who wanted to discuss a position as associate project director. After the usual small talk and fencing, I was hired for considerably more money than I'd made at Chilton.

The work was varied and responsible, and I found myself more committed to the job. Regular paychecks meant we were able to eat out more, replace outmoded clothes, and save a little besides. Meanwhile Juneau seemed edgy, but I had no idea how close to the brink she felt. She recalls her state of mind at the time . . .

The cross-country trip left my nerves frayed. Now a simple car ride was a terrifying experience. I was sure David was going to kill me in an accident. At times I even thought he wanted to.

Our nomadic life was taking its toll. I felt like I had no anchor. That's when I began to hate David, certain he didn't love me. One day I woke up, and the apartment seemed foggy. It was as if everything was covered by a mist. I looked at David through the watery haze with a heart filled with scorn, and thought: I'm in hell. I need help. I can't go on like this, life is too horrible!

I went into group therapy at Cedars-Sinai to try to save myself from destruction, and to understand why I was so miserable. The sessions didn't seem to help, but they did drive me to look for other ways to solve my problem. I knew other people couldn't do it for me; I had to find the answer inside. That, I sensed, meant a spiritual search. Yet the Bible, a

church, or a pastor never entered my mind as a
possible solution.

Instead I haunted the public library, reading
Eastern mystics and self-realization gurus, looking
for a method to search my inner self, get free of this
miserable existence, and find some kind of peace. I
found a few clues on how to meditate and pieced
together bits of various techniques in my efforts to
quiet my churning brain. It seemed to help a little.

Then I found a job teaching arts and crafts at
a convalescent hospital. My self-esteem grew a
little. David was wrapped up in his ambitions
and had little awareness of my pain.

Watching TV one Sunday night, we were shocked when
Ed Sullivan introduced his star act as "the newest sensation
from England, now taking the world by storm!" It was the
Beatles, singing the same dumb "I Wanna Hold Your Hand"
that British teenagers had been raving over a few years earlier. Sullivan's audience squealed just as mightily over the
young men with Prince Valiant haircuts—and both of us remained just as unimpressed.

"I still don't know what they're cheering about," Juneau
said.

"It's the hair," I replied. "Give 'em a crew cut, and they'd
be out of business."

One night the phone rang. On the line was British author Christopher Isherwood, whose book *Goodbye to Berlin*
became the classic stage musical *Cabaret*. Weeks before I'd
written him a fan letter on his novel *Down There on a Visit,*
and intrigued by my comments, he wanted to meet me. So I
invited him over to our place.

In honor of his visit, Juneau scoured our modest apartment, and I bought a bottle of fine French wine. Unhappily,
there was nothing much we could do about the drab court
and neighborhood we lived in. At exactly 8:00 P.M., the ap-
pointed time, Isherwood rang our bell, and Juneau let him
in. He was short and lean, and his boyish manner, tinted

sandy hair, open blue eyes, and erect posture made him seem more like forty-eight than his actual sixty years.

Awed by his reputation, I broke out the wine to loosen things a bit.

"If you don't mind, I'd prefer fruit juice," he said.

He settled for a soft drink, and we spent the next hour exploring the theme of spiritual search so dominant in most of his later writings. Then he got into his true passion; he was a disciple of the Hindu monk Swami Prabhavananda. Isherwood detested the Christianity he'd been raised in because of its "stilted morality." To the Hindus, though, God was Self and sin simply a hindrance to human spiritual progress, contrasted to the Christian notion of offenses against a personal God.

"We're really all part of an all-encompassing essence," he explained. "That's why what we do to others we really do to ourselves. Good or bad, we bless or judge ourselves. What we think of as our individual Self is really the same Self as everyone else has, and this Self contains infinite knowledge and infinite joy."

"It sounds as though you're saying we are God," I said.

"That's exactly right," he said, smiling. "And so we are!"

"Then who created us?" Juneau asked.

"It's a moot point," he replied. "It really doesn't matter who made us, and all the speculation in the world can't bring us any closer to the reality. But we can know who God is by merely learning to know ourselves, you see!"

The esoteric thoughts made my head swim and I had to cover my mouth from several nervous yawns. Soon we'd exhausted our capacities for Hindu theology, and Isherwood politely asked about my own writings. Briefly filling him in on our English adventures, we ran out of things to talk about. Clearly, we were not candidates for his homosexual circle or potential disciples for his swami, the overriding interests of his life. When he left, we spent the hours before sleep speculating about the affinity many homosexuals have for Eastern religions and New Age philosophy, systems that do not conflict with their life style. As Isherwood himself framed it, "The Christian God is a Superboss who condemns sin and demands obedience. That's no sort of God for me."

By June we felt settled enough to think about buying our first house. Our hearts yearned to stay in Santa Monica, but a few visits to local realtors persuaded us to look farther out where prices were more affordable. The nearest suburbs were in the San Fernando Valley. Ed Tickner and our other show-biz friends advised against it, citing the Valley's reputation as a middle-class enclave of losers and working people. But hanging around with guitar twangers had no appeal for us, so off to the Valley Juneau went, doing all the work of checking out listings, visiting likely places, and hassling out preliminary terms. Finally, she was ready for me.

One Saturday afternoon a real estate agent drove us to a two-bedroom house in Encino. The place was not much bigger than our motel cottage, and it was painted a nauseous pale green that gave it all the appeal of a can of pea soup. But it had a fully fenced back yard with its own fountain, plus an utterly charming detached cottage sided by elm trees. The owner offered us a lease option, so we could live there a year before deciding to buy. If we did, some of our rent would be applied to the down payment. That did it. We wrote out a check covering first and last month's rent, repacked the VW, and made the San Fernando Valley our home.

The suburban lifestyle was balm to our souls as we settled into steady, predictable patterns. I found my research job challenging as I directed a variety of studies: death and burial for Forest Lawn, pet owners and feeding for Purina, the Scandinavian image in America for AB Platmanufaktur of Stockholm.

Juneau began painting, spurred by her job as art therapist for Brentwood Convalescent Hospital, and she continued her group psychotherapy at Cedars-Sinai. Efforts to understand herself gave her insights into me . . .

David was an angry young man. Angry at the publishing world for not recognizing his talents. These big editors were his gods who did not return his worship with blessings of fame and wealth.

We argued daily over anything and everything— how we would raise our child that we both knew we'd never have, how we'd build our imaginary mansion in the mountains. I'd placed some pieces of sculpture with a Ventura Boulevard art gallery, but the low prices I got for my long hours of work discouraged me.

One day I tuned to a radio talk program where the host was touting a record teaching meditation. Finally, *I* thought, *I'd learn how to do it properly. It took a few months to save enough money to pay for the record and a phonograph to play it on. Meanwhile I listened to the show for instructions I might try until I had the record. This seemed the magical tool I was looking for, the one that would straighten out my life and make me a contented, happy person. I even stopped going to group therapy, knowing I'd soon be saved by meditation.*

Finally, I had saved enough and went down to the Foundation of Human Understanding to buy the record. While there I met Roy Masters, the creator of the record, who was curt and abrupt to me. Though he hurt my feelings, I thought I deserved his rudeness since he'd been meditating for years and could see into people. After listening to his record a few times, I began meditating on my own. His English accent echoed in my head, and afraid something or someone might take over my body, I fought to stay alert.

Meditating twice a day and even more often, I was disappointed that nothing inside me seemed to change. Where were the great psychological truths that were supposed to pop into my head? I began listening to the radio show more often, seeking clues for what I was doing wrong. Slowly over time I noticed I was getting a little control over my emotions, mostly because his record stressed the listener to have patience, kindness, *and* understanding. *So I stopped arguing with David, letting him have the last word, and our home became more peaceful.*

While Juneau was into self-help, I was bursting with new creativity. With plenty of energy left over for night and weekend writing, I began a comic novel based on my Mexican adventures, sold four chapters as short stories to men's magazines, wrote and published other stories and poetry, and joined the Authors Guild of the Authors League of America.

The tranquillity was upset one morning on the Hollywood freeway when the driver in front of me hit his power brakes and stopped on a dime. I responded by braking as hard as I could but had to watch in horror as my front end plowed into his rear bumper. The formalities of exchanging license numbers and insurance agents proceeded amicably, and the cop who called in a tow truck for the VW was most cordial. But it meant a black mark on my driving record, a jump in our insurance premium, and the need to buy a new car.

Our mourning ended the moment we pulled out of the car lot with a snappy blue Datsun sedan. It symbolized a brand-new start from all we had left behind—including Old World European aesthetics and East Coast cynicism. Happy days were here at last, we thought.

9

Dress Rehearsal for Oblivion

The serenity was simply a lull in the storm. Black rights protests and the escalating Vietnam War stoked the political flames, and we began subscribing to the underground publications then springing up—*Ramparts* magazine, the *L.A. Free Press* and *Berkeley Barb*. They advocated a vastly different kind of politics from our Kennedy liberalism, as they saw the whole world as a web of interlocking conspiracies. America as world imperialism's "Mother Country" was painted with the darkest brush of all. The underground press included enough hard facts in their reporting to make it seem convincing, and in the mood of the times, we were ready to believe the worst.

My only brother was buried in Belgium, near the place he was killed in the Battle of the Bulge. I was not a pacifist, but my standards for giving one's last measure of devotion in warfare were tough ones. The more we learned about the Vietnam War, the less zeal we felt. And from Washington, something began to smell very rotten.

Other people were coming to similar conclusions. We started going to rallies and teach-ins where we listened to rehashes of what we'd read in the underground press. The same leaders kept showing up everywhere, including big-bellied Jesuit priest Blaise Bompane replete with vestments and UCLA professor Donald Freed.

Drugs, mostly marijuana, were passed around at these gatherings to make the dialectic more endurable—the same anti-imperialist, military-industrial, race-mongering diatribes we'd heard back in England. As the crowds began to swell, folk singers like Phil Ochs and Joan Baez began showing up. Juneau and I joined lots of coalitions with ten words in their title, paid dues and attended enough meetings to see that all these groups were being run by the same half-dozen leaders pounding us with the same relentless Marxist viewpoint.

In Michigan, Tom Hayden and his Students for a Democratic Society group organized the first "Mobilization Against the War," a series of rallies that brought the movement media coverage and credibility. Hayden and his people were using the finger-wrist-arm method to bring their Socialist utopia to America: "Give me a finger, and I'll take a wrist; give me a wrist, and I'll take your arm." Though by now Juneau and I suspected these antiwar "leaders" were hardworking Marxists exploiting a situation, the cause seemed right enough to ignore their motives. And rally by rally, protest by protest, our numbers grew and our chants for peace louder and more impressive.

Thanksgiving week a petition was sent to all 7,500 members of the Authors Guild, inviting us to put our bylines to work in the cause of peace. A short statement "earnestly petitioned the President and the Congress" to declare a cease-fire in Vietnam, press for an international settlement to end the war and, once reached, to bring our boys back home. Juneau and I discussed the risks. We knew the CIA and FBI were busy amassing detailed files on activists, and this petition would surely get their notice. But the wording amounted to little more than urging our government to settle the war at the conference table instead of the battlefield.

The next day I signed it and sent it back, expecting all but a handful of timid souls would do likewise. Early in the new year, the petition was published in full-page newspaper ads all over the country. It contained just 534 names, a few of them established by-lines like Albert Maltz of "Hollywood 10" fame, actress Dody Goodman, Dr. Benjamin Spock, Gloria Steinem, Studs Terkel, Joseph Heller, Rona Jaffe, Rod Serling, and Terry Southern. Over 7,000 others—including Norman Mailer and James Baldwin among an army of "big names"—were conspicuous by their absence, unwilling to put their careers behind their mouths.

As the fires of war blazed red hot, the spirit of Armageddon permeated the land. The apocalyptic mood created hunger for new drugs and a search for mystical power to save oneself from the onrushing holocaust. The tribal gatherings called be-ins, love-ins, and happenings occurred almost every weekend. While "straights" raised families and kept faith with LBJ, we "hip ones" were turning on with drugs, meeting weekly at large open-air gatherings, and drawing strength in our mushrooming numbers.

Workshops were held on college and university campuses or at churches—invariably Unitarian, Quaker and other liberal denominations. Nothing less than blatant indoctrination sessions, they were run by internationalists like Blaise Bompane and Donald Freed who blamed the problems of the world on big-business neo-imperialism. Portraying the U.S. government as a blood-hungry monster oppressing the poor people of the world, they carefully drew distinctions between the "generous big-hearted American people" and those "warmongers in the Pentagon and White House." Whenever the Soviet Union or its puppet states entered the discussion, their zeal to defend Marxist-Leninist countries at first offended us, but they were so blatantly predictable we soon grew numb to it. Our goal was to end the war honorably, and if others had broader aims, we'd just cooperate where our interests meshed and ignore all the rest—so we thought.

------------------------------♦------------------------------

About this time Timothy Leary, the Harvard professor turned drug guru, was going around preaching LSD as the ultimate answer to all the world's problems. Already predisposed to trying it because of Hal Galili's selling job in England, we felt it would be a key to open our self-understanding. So we applied to join Leary's LSD group—League for Spiritual Discovery—where we could take the stuff under "controlled supervision."

In midsummer Susan Leary called to tell me the League had no chapter in southern California, but Timothy would be in California shortly and might initiate a chapter then. She sent us a one-page form asking for "location of shrine," "devotional symbols," "favorite mantras," and other quasi-religious particulars, ending in a pledge never to reveal the names of other league members. We filled it in and returned it with a check.

A week later we got a manual in the mail, written by Leary but based on the Egyptian *Book of the Dead*. In it he described the stages of an LSD trip, explaining how the "spirit" goes through various stages of freeing itself from the bonds of flesh. At the climax of the experience, he wrote, the ego dies temporarily to its earthly conditioning—presenting the voyager with a moment of truth. Now comes the time to be "reborn" by visualizing a great personality and striving to identify with that personage. When the chemical intoxication wears off, Leary promised, it would leave behind the impress of our new identity. After a series of such "reprogramming" sessions—number not specified—we'd turn into a living image of Jesus, Buddha, Mahatma Gandhi, or whoever else we chose to clone. Since Juneau had dropped group therapy after not achieving the peace she sought, we were both wide open to try Leary's way.

The idea of surrendering total control to a mind-blowing drug was, I confess, pretty scary—but when measured against the high adventure of a new experience, we were chomping at the bit to try it. One Tuesday night about ten, the phone rang.

"Is this David? asked a familiar tenor voice. It was Leary himself.

"Sure is!" I said. "Dr. Leary?"

"Yes, I'm in San Francisco. I'll be down in southern California next week. If you're available, I'd like to meet you and your wife. Have you ever taken lysergic acid diethylamide before?"

"No, never."

"Good, we prefer it that way. How's next Wednesday, say four in the afternoon?"

"Fine, I'll take off early from work."

"What sort of work do you do?"

"Marketing research."

"Oho, a mind bender, eh? We'll soon cure you of that!"

We laughed together, and I gave him directions to our house. With each passing day, tension grew more fierce. Tuesday night Juneau and I couldn't get to sleep. The next day at work I found it impossible to concentrate. Promptly at three, I made my excuse and took off for home. Then began the vigil, peering out our front windows for Leary's car. But when four came and went, then five and six, the fire went out. The great psychedelic doctor and his *tune-in, turn-on, drop-out* ministry had stood us up.

Venting our disappointment on Leary and his cursed league, we licked our ego wounds and had our first good night's sleep in days. When we opened the morning *Times* to read about a drug arrest involving Leary and several associates at a home in Santa Barbara, feelings of rejection vanished. Our initiation had only been delayed, not canceled.

Inspired by Juneau, I became interested in the idea of mind-body control. A weekly program on KPFK radio called "The Mystic Circle" taught listeners how to use mental imagery, relaxation, Taoist breathing, and other means to achieve "cosmic consciousness." The moderator, Professor Jack Gariss, talked his audience through the process using on-air imagery. We enjoyed playing his mind game along with the feeling of controlling our own bodies, health, and well-being.

Juneau had discovered another radio talk show called "Your Moment of Truth," hosted by a transplanted Englishman with a cockney accent named Roy Masters. Masters offered advice to people who called in complaining of personal problems, but his relentlessly know-it-all manner really turned me off. Lecturing callers about their defects, he invariably blamed all their ills on hidden anger. Anger, he insisted, was the primal evil behind every bad thing that happens to people—insanity, disease, sexual hang-ups, drug addiction, and death. His solution? His own brand of meditation called Psycho-catalysis, available on an LP record for $5.95.

Juneau had bought it, and after awhile I noticed she'd grown more calm. She was more inward and—to my way of thinking—more smug and less caring. Challenged and curious, I tuned into Masters a few times during lunch hour on my car radio. When I heard him tell one caller he (Masters) was "beyond sin, mortal weakness, and even death," I had my justification. When I came home that night, I told Juneau to stop meditating the Roy Masters way because it was bound to mess her up. Explaining what I'd heard, I made a persuasive case for his being an egomaniac on the loose, and she accepted my arguments.

———————◆———————

It was spring, the season when young men's hearts turn to thoughts of romance and writers think of pushing book projects. With the neobeatnik renaissance in full swing, it struck me as good publishing sense to put out a mass-market title catering to all those young rebels. So I sent out letters to a half-dozen top paperback publishers in New York to share my views and give them the good news that just such a book, *The Century God Slept*, happened to be available from A. S. Barnes. Before long, I hit pay dirt. The weird thing about it was that I reaped where I had not sown.

A letter from Jerry Gross, editor of Paperback Library, informed me he'd bought reprint rights from A. S. Barnes and would be publishing a mass edition of *The Century God Slept* in September. With the hippy phenomenon in full bloom, Gross wondered if I could go up to San Francisco, suck up background and color, then do another book on youth, drugs, sex and rebellion circa 1967? They wanted it out by summer 1968, so I'd have to get cracking and finish my manuscript by March. Paperback Library was one firm I had not contacted, but why look a gift horse in the mouth?

Like a stallion too long in pasture, I broke into a wild gallop. Summer is slow season in the research business, so it was easy to arrange time off. Juneau helped me dress the part, as I prepared to live the hippy life in the Haight-Ashbury. Since my hair was longish to begin with, we just let my locks grow more wavy. Though over thirty, I looked younger, and I already knew most of the "hip" phrases in current vogue. We bought a pair of candy-striped bell-bottom jeans, some colorful psychedelic shirts, and all-purpose boots. Juneau added wooden beads, a thick leather wristwatch band, and an elastic money belt she made from a cast-off stocking, and my costume was set. Early one morning in June, I kissed Juneau good-bye and boarded a Greyhound bus to San Francisco. My luggage—a rolled sleeping bag and a canvas shoulder purse—drew contemptuous sneers from my fellow passengers and made me feel more secure in my adopted hippy role.

Late that afternoon, we got out at the dumpy downtown station. Since I hadn't been to San Francisco for two years and had read about all the radical changes, I was disappointed to see it looking so unchanged. Business suits still abounded, housewives still paraded down Market Street on shopping tours, and all the longhaired freaks I'd expected to find were nowhere in sight. I was hungry and bus-weary but decided to hold off eating until I got to the Haight-Ashbury so I could take my first meal among the natives.

I hopped a bus, and as we crossed Divisadero Street, faces turned from white to black, brown and tan. Then, suddenly, we entered a place where bodies overflowed both sidewalks, reducing our bus speed to a crawl.

Crowds of young people paraded by dressed in curious costumes snitched from old cellar trunks, reflecting the influence of cowboy movies, newsclips of Nehru, the space race, and thermonuclear terror. The faces looked surprisingly serene, eyes clear, soft, nonviolent, lost in psychedelic peace. Marking a big shift from the uptight beatniks I'd known back East, they struck me as a gathering of gentle dropouts, losers, runaways, rejected kids, and neophyte saints heralding the death of the old earth and preparing the planet for the New Age. Sensing there was more here than just drugs, sex, and rebellion, I aimed to find out what it was.

I ate a hamburger dinner at Bob's Drive-In and went looking for a place to stay. At a storefront realtor on Haight, the lady showed me a book listing vastly overpriced rooms. I thanked her and went back to the streets. A stoned guitarist seated in a doorway told me about "The Switchboard," a phone referral service for everything available in the area. They gave me the number of a "crashpad" hosted by "Amy," and when I called, a woman told me to come right over.

The pad was a brick-front row house with heavily curtained windows on all three floors. The staircase was pitch dark. Groping my way up to the second floor, I knocked at the specified door. Nobody stirred, so I hit it twice more and it opened. There stood a woman my own age with the most striking sea-green eyes I'd ever seen. The rest of her—long dark hair, high cheekbones, full lips and figure—did nothing to damage the first impression.

"You're the boy who called about crashing?" she asked.

"Right. And you must be Amy."

"No, I'm Thais. And you are . . . ?"

"David."

"My favorite name. Can I get you tea or coffee?"

"Anything sounds good."

Stepping in, I found myself in a twenty-foot-square room lit by a dim red lamp and fluorescent black light. The walls and ceiling glowed with posters, Oriental designs, and a huge Uncle Sam pointing his accusing military finger at me. Mattresses and pillows covered the floor. While I waited, a musical Hare Krishna chant blasted out of hidden speakers. A few minutes later, the woman came back carrying a tray and set a cup before me.

We sat awhile drinking tea, and she laid out the house rules. "The front door locks at midnight weekdays, two o'clock weekends. Welcome to the new San Francisco!"

Unrolling my sleeping bag, I stretched out, munched a cookie, and got lost in the glowing patterns on the ceiling.

Before I knew it, I was asleep. Started awake by a stereo din of amplified guitars, thundering drums, and tinkling tambourines, I sat up. The floor was filled with bodies, some of them coupled off and cuddling. A young black man wearing earphones came over to me.

"Can you dig this?" he asked, handing me the headset.

I slipped them over my head and was immediately immersed in a rock universe of magnified tones and overtones, reverberating into my head and heart. It was so intense it was painful, and I soon returned them to the fellow.

"That's really something," I said.

"Outta sight is more like it," he said.

The talk around me centered mostly on drugs—the best, the strongest, and where to get them—interspersed with reminiscences of back-home romances and tales of run-ins with the law. Most of the kids were under twenty so the room was replete with "Wow," "Groovy," and "Can you dig it?" It soon grew clear that these were new arrivals like myself, crashing here until they could find permanent digs in collective apartments or shared rooms. Listening to the buzz of eager young voices, I nodded off again and slept till daybreak when I rolled up my sleeping bag and slipped out.

After a donuts-and-coffee breakfast at Tracy's Cafe where I chatted with a couple of Hell's Angels, I made a grand tour of the district. It was an eye-popping revelation. A free clinic run by a young doctor named Smith dispensed no-charge medicine and treatment to anyone asking for it. There were "free stores" where anyone could take anything from clothes to appliances and tools for no charge. They were run by a group calling itself The Diggers, and each item was stamped with a circle formed by a snake eating its own tail and the word WE printed in the center. An accompanying flyer explained that the object was "part of the public domain. It belongs to everyone. No form of contract, exchange of money or goods, incantation or ritual can transform it back into 'private property.' Use it awhile and pass it on to someone else. Abolish some private property today!"

There were Aquarian Age curio shops selling meditational products, head shops offering drug accessories and incense, macrobiotic restaurants serving startling varieties of vegetarian fare, and a UFO sensory show combining lights and full-volume sound to trip out the human mind for twenty-five cents. There were leather shops, craft centers, book barns, coffee bars, munchy stores, love bazaars—all geared to satisfy new consumer tastes shaped through the lens of psychedelic drugs.

More astonishing than the Haight shopping center, though, were the hordes of zonked-out young people moving along both sidewalks of the five-block village in a perennial parade, admiring one another's zany dress, eager to share their food, drugs, and affection with perfect strangers.

Small groups of actors from the Mime Theater performed living plays, pushing the same share-love-abolish-private-property themes. Still others challenged passersby to debates, gathering crowds to listen to the discourse. There was so much going on I hated to stay too long at any one scene because there might be another one even more compelling just ahead.

The word went out on the street that the Grateful Dead rock group, appearing nightly at the Fillmore West Theater, was giving a free concert at Hippy Hill in Golden Gate Park. Following the crowds, I found a gentle grassy slope where a sea of blankets, youngsters, clanking tambourines, and bongos created a thrumming roar like a thunderstorm. Settling down on the grass, I soon was invited to join a group. The Dead never did show up, but nobody really cared. I met a bunch of young folks, some my own age and a few much older. As each hour went on, I felt my ambition-driven personality begin to mellow out.

That afternoon I found a room for ten dollars a week and settled in to continue my research. Soon I developed a pattern, spending most of my time at the places that most satisfied my interests: the I and Thou coffee bar featuring nightly poetry readings with jazz accompaniment; the God's Eye Theater where gurus, preachers, and cosmic messiahs argued the merits of their faith; Hippy Hill where the gentle tribes gathered every afternoon; and free communal meals along the grassy strip fronting Golden Gate Park, where The

Diggers served stew, bread, and salad made from supermarket castoffs while politicos recruited newcomers, promoted stop-the-war actions, and passed around endless petitions.

Over time I made friends with Larry, a sheet-metal worker from Pittsburgh who ran the God's Eye Theater; Hershy, who sold jewelry and gave anticapitalist speeches every day at the park over his portable sound system; David, a young black aspiring jazz musician; Shooky, a teenage runaway from New York; Betty, a thirteen-year-old Iowa farm girl who was sleeping with every draft evader she could find; Penny, who had escaped from a cult commune—and a hundred others who shared their stories with me. Taking voluminous notes and collecting artifacts, flyers, and vivid memories, I realized there was no way to assimilate all I was experiencing and write a novel in the six months demanded for a Paperback Library "quickie."

One evening when I was standing in front of the Fillmore with David, a wide-eyed young man came by selling a stash of Owsley Purples—the most potent form of LSD yet made in the people's labs. Having never tried it, I seized the chance to buy two dozen tabs for two dollars each. I offered to share it with David.

"Wow, man, you don't know what you're asking," he said. "Grass is cool, speed has its place, but acid and me just don't groove together."

"Everyone is raving about what a great trip acid is."

"Maybe for some, but not this dude. Hey, let me know how you make out."

About eight that night, I couldn't wait to get back to my room. Swallowing one of the Owsley Purples, I turned out the lights, lit a candle, sat by the kitchen table, and waited. Nothing happened for the longest time until I thought I'd been hustled, paying forty-eight dollars for sugar pills. Then a twitch of nervous energy exploded at the base of my skull. Everything held still awhile, and then my body seemed to turn to Jell-O. The candlelight flared like a Roman candle, a surge of warm taffy flooded my chest, and a bolt hit the center of my brain so it felt like a squeezed fist had been forced through my skull. A warm lavalike substance flowed through my whole body in undulating waves, and I lost the sense of who I was. The thought struck me I was dying.

"Oooohhhh, aaaahhhh, owwwwwwwww!" a small voice cried.

I realized it was me, my voice, but *I* no longer existed. It was the most terrifying feeling I'd ever had, and for what seemed a timeless span I heard groaning, moaning, prayers, and pleas for the thing to end. But there was no stopping it. I heard crazy laughter, too, and babbling until I feared the taffy stuff flooding my body would somehow pour out of an orifice and I would be emptied and dead like a fly sucked dry by a spider. Who would tell Juneau, and what would she do? I tried walking around, but I was so unsteady I lurched drunkenly against the wall, ending face down on the carpet to writhe against a serpentine force inside. Colors exploded in my head, and suddenly I was lost in a vision of floating space, stars and free-flow nothingness.

It was almost daybreak when the stuff wore off enough so I could go out. David, I concluded, was right. The only way to take the stuff was in a controlled setting. I'd take it back with me, read Leary's book more carefully, and do it with Juneau according to expert advice.

When it was time to leave San Francisco I had the definite feeling that some secret was buried in all the bizarre madness, the secret that would give me the answer to everything. Saying good-bye to my new friends, I vowed to return and headed home just as I'd come—glared at and whispered about in a Greyhound bus.

———————————— ♦ ————————————

Juneau and I wasted no time getting started on our LSD pilgrimage. Both of us reread Leary's *Book of the Dead* from cover to cover, made notes, and proceeded to follow his directions explicitly—except for the sex he advocated. Because Juneau was afraid she'd be too vulnerable, we added our own rules, which included no undressing or touching while under the drug's influence. Every Friday after our work week, we'd prepare our house, stack baroque LP's on our turntable, set up candles, and lock all the doors. After pulling down the blinds, with fear and trembling we'd swallow our Owsley Purples and wait. And we were never disappointed. In the course of the next eight hours, give or take a few, we would consistently experience, week after week, a huge dose of hell on earth. Juneau lost five pounds every Friday night and gained three back the next few days.

Saturday nights we'd discuss what could have gone wrong, then go back to the book and try changing the settings and music. But next time out the results were exactly the same. Finally, after our eleventh session when all our Owsleys were gone, we gave it up as a dead loss. Leary's "sacrament" was our poison.

"Maybe," Juneau suggested, "we're not as far gone as he is."

But LSD by no means exhausted our search for a Higher Something. A friend who was into Eastern mysticism introduced us to an American-born Buddhist monk living on a Los Angeles mountaintop. His name was French McClellan Moore, a lean, blue-eyed man in his sixties with a flowing white beard and saffron robe. He had set up a temple in his home, and one evening we took part in a "meditation" group.

When we arrived, Moore was seated cross-legged on the floor before an altar adorned with metal objects, engravings, candelabra, and plastic fruit. His head was bowed, and he remained in a prayerful pose for some ten minutes. When he lifted his head at last, his eyes were glazed and faraway.

"So glad you could come," he said, coming over to shake our hands. His fingers were long, slender, and oddly cold.

There were just five of us, so he had us sit in a circle, hold hands, and hum "ommmmmm" in unison. It set up a buzzing in our ears, but despite our willingness to be transfigured, all we felt was sweat forming in our palms and a sense of foolishness. Moore quickly read our mood and, ending the omming, suggested we retire to another room. There he turned on a flicker box and a strobe machine creating illusions in light, space and shape.

Soon we felt lightheaded and unreal, but certainly nothing to base a faith on. As though reading our thoughts, Moore leaned over and put his hands on our shoulders.

"I'd like to invite you to a special service this Sunday," he said. "It's at Griffith Park, and we'll be sharing a very powerful sacrament."

"What sort of sacrament?" Juneau asked.

Moore's blue eyes twinkled playfully. "If I told you, it wouldn't be a surprise. Please come. You won't regret it."

We hadn't intended to go, but the promise of a "special sacrament" intrigued us. That Sunday at the park we found Moore in his cross-legged stance, omming with a small group of young seekers and an older American Indian. Looking up, he gave us a big welcome and bade us join his circle. Without preamble, he reached into a basket and came out with a pint milk bottle filled with yellow liquid. A long stirring rod and a straw protruded from it.

"Before we start, please move in closer," he said in an odd high-pitched voice. "Come here by me so we can be closer for the partaking of the sacrament."

We did as he asked, huddling in on the altar, the religious objects, and the bottle. Moore slowly stirred the thick liquid.

"I've used a number of sacred herbs and substances," he said. "And for taste, there's a base of lemon custard. It helps it all go down smoother."

"What else do you have in there?" the Indian asked suspiciously.

Moore never answered. Instead he placed the straw in his mouth and continued to stir sensuously, all eyes trained on the swirling liquid.

"I suggest you take three small sips of the sacrament," he finally said. "Three sips, small sips, or you might get too much. Perhaps if you all watched me—like so!"

He set the straw to his lips and sucked. The fluid level fell slightly, as he sucked again. The last was longest, emptying almost an inch of the bottle's level. Then he passed the bottle around. I thought the stuff tasted like custard mixed with olive oil.

"Good! Wonderful!" Moore cried. "Now let's join hands for an introductory chant."

We linked hands, and Moore started omming soft and low, gradually rising to a crescendo like a haywire short-wave radio. The rest of us joined in self-consciously until the weird sound filled the air.

A wondrous calm spread in warm waves from my belly out. "Very nice," I said, but my tongue was lazy and the words slurred. The Indian next to me had a silly grin on his face. Juneau's eyes were closed, and her face looked peaceful.

"What's in that drink?" the Indian asked.

"It's best I don't tell you at this time," Moore replied. "Man thrives in mystery. But I can tell you there's a large combination of active ingredients, all adding their own special power." He reached over, grabbed a gray metal object, and held it up for everyone to see. "Do you know what this is?"

A few of us mumbled no.

"It's a dorje," he said, turning it in his fingers. "The dorje is a magical implement. In India they call it the thunderbolt of Buddha. He who holds the dorje with the proper attitude becomes filled with its power, all the power of the universe—OMMMMMMMMMMMMMMMM!"

Led by the older man's electronic humming, we launched into a huge, overwhelming chorus of the great mindless OMMMMMMAAANEEEE OOMMMMMMMMMMM! Time disappeared as our consciousness centered on the chant.

My inner vision was locked onto an infinite golden band speckled with blood-red dots. I tried mightily to open my eyes and managed a brief glance at the Indian fellow beside me. His eyes were closed so profoundly he looked dead, and with great effort I raised my hand to nudge his shoulder. His eyes came open then—blurry, swimming, filmy—and all he could say was "Woowwwwww!" before the eyes closed again.

I started to check out the others, but Moore launched another OMMMMM that pulled me back into paralyzing darkness. My will to resist was gone. All emotion was dead. Suddenly, I had a vision that my being was reduced to a blue-white light around which danced three identical sparks. Then my spark turned into a great muscular heart with blood oozing from its center. The blood grew thicker, running, seeping as my life flowed out of my chest. The thought of death brought me out.

As I forced my eyes open, a dull ache filled my chest. Hovering over our circle was a white-haired woman in a miniskirt. Her face was thick with makeup, giving her the appearance of an ancient kewpie doll. A group of Japanese tourists leaned over us, snapping pictures of the "American Buddhists." Moore was staring at me, eyes wide as saucers. I was struck with the realization that this was some kind of satanic rite and I'd been chosen as its sacrificial lamb.

Just then Juneau pointed to a rock beside her and said, "Look at the blood coming out of the rock!"

I couldn't see it, but I knew she was seeing it clearly.

"How do you feel?" Moore asked me in a strained tone.

"You ——!" I growled. "You're trying to kill me, you and your pack of witches!"

"It's all right," he purred. "Just take it easy."

"Easy? You think dying is easy? Wait until it's your turn!"

I realized my words sounded crazy, but they made perfect sense to me and—I believed—to Moore. Struggling to my feet, I swayed a few seconds feeling totally drained of will and energy. But I managed to get to Juneau and pull her up.

I started away with Juneau, and Moore called, "You're betraying me! You've hurt me!" I glanced back to see him clutching his heart, even as the ache vanished from my own chest. We staggered across the knoll to the parking lot and drove off. The freeway ride was totally surreal, like a bad dream with cars swirling past and around us. Juneau clutched at my arm, sure we'd be smashed at any moment. I shared her fear but kept going. Miraculously, we arrived home without mishap.

We made black coffee and, as we sipped, rehashed the event. Juneau had seen the same yellow band with red dots, and she had the identical vision of my bleeding heart. We felt lucky just to be alive.

It took two days before the full effects wore off. The newspaper weather page reported Sunday had been the apex of the full moon, the time of witches' celebrations and satanic sacrifice. During the week we both grew more incensed at being drugged by that fake Buddhist priest. The following Sunday we returned to Griffith Park, planning to confront him. Moore wasn't there, but we did run into the Indian fellow, who greeted us like long-lost family.

"Hey, that was some stuff!" he remarked.

"Ready for more?" I quipped.

"You kidding? Hey, never again! Say, did you see what I saw?"

"Like what? The speckled golden ribbon?"

"Yeah! And how about the bloody heart? Hey, man, was that your heart they were eating?"

"Yes," I replied. "And I hope they get themselves a good case of indigestion."

10

Searching for the Truth

When an author has a book published, he usually sweats out the weeks until the first copies appear in the bookstores. That wasn't the way it happened this time.

Late one September afternoon, while Juneau was buying shampoo at a Thrifty Drugstore, I was checking out the paperback books. One cover displaying a young couple in mod clothes grabbed my attention, and the title lead-in strengthened the attraction—"Tune in, turn on, and drop out with . . . *Like Now!*" I pulled it out for a better look. Like a lightning bolt, the author's name flashed at my eyes—it was me! Microscopic print under *Like Now!* read "(original title: *The Century God Slept*)."

Momentarily peeved that the publisher hadn't even told me about the title change, my irritation quickly dissolved before the excitement of an eye-catching cover design and graphics compelling enough to make my hand reach out for it. If I did, we reasoned, so would lots more. Fired up, we made the rounds of the big supermarkets and drug chains—they all had copies on display. We were in business!

Five days later, I checked back at the markets near work to find only one copy left at one, the rest all sold out. The same was true in Encino. A few days later new piles of *Like Now!*s were back on display and again sold like gangbusters,

143

moving much faster than highly publicized releases with movie tie-ins and multimillion dollar promotions. I felt vindicated and we envisioned a great big people's best seller in paperback. Then up jumped the devil.

A friend, Betty Larsen, called to complain that she could not get the book at her nearby Gelson's Market. The manager told her he had sold out. He asked the distributor for more but had been turned down. This was three weeks to the day from its first being offered for sale. I stopped by a bookstore near work to buy a copy for John Logue, but there were none to be had. The owner said he'd already put in a reorder but so far no books. He'd remind the wholesaler rep at his next visit in two days. When I returned, the man grew redfaced when I asked about my order.

"Dunno when they might come in," he mumbled. "It's a funny business the paperback trade."

A few days later Betty called again, all excited because Gelson's store manager had a copy for her. Strangely, though, he had the book in his office desk. It wasn't out on the racks for sale or displayed anywhere in the store. Nor could we find a single copy anywhere in Los Angeles! Juneau called the distributor, who justified his unwillingness to restock his outlets when they sold out.

"You know the kind of book it is, one of those hippy books," he carped. "I can't promise to put any more into Gelson's for you. If I do, they won't be on the racks. I'll leave them with the manager and you can buy one from him."

We never again saw a book displayed for sale anywhere. A few bookshops kept copies hidden under the checkout counter, but for all practical purposes it had disappeared. Complaints to my publisher went nowhere, since they readily accepted the right of distributors to do as they pleased.

I called on book buyers for the drug and supermarket chains. They told me they'd had no customer complaints about my book. In fact, they'd been doing brisk business with it and would be glad to have it back in stock.

"If you want to get to the bottom of this, talk to Bob Derry at Sunset News," one advised. "He's the guy with all the power."

The same thing was happening all over the country, according to the publisher's sales director. "There have been no reorders from any wholesalers anywhere, even though they sold out their first orders in a few weeks," he wrote. That infuriated me so I dropped in on Sunset News downtown, the paperback distributor for southern California. Bob Derry was gone for the day.

It took two days before I found Derry in at his warehouse. A fiftyish ex-con type with a mashed nose, blue-eyed slits, and scar tissue brows, he wasted no time trying to bum-rush me out the door.

"You think these are books?" he snarled. "These ain't books. These are magazines. Ten days and they're history so out they go!"

"I checked out the books you stock for the markets," I said. "Lots of them are four or five years old."

He didn't say anything for the longest time. When he looked up, his eyes had all but disappeared.

"Listen, Chagall," he hissed. "We know who you are. We know where you live. Lay off if you know what's good for you!"

That sobered me. When I got home, I told Juneau what had happened, and she wasted no time giving me her considered opinion.

"Is it worth a bomb under your car hood?" she asked.

I found her logic impeccable and so ended our impromptu investigation of the paperback industry. Soon after that a letter arrived from Jerry Gross. "I can't be too optimistic about your novel-in-progress on the Haight-Ashbury scene. The times they are a changin' as the song goes, and I don't think the hippies are long for this world. So I can't promise even that the theme will meet with approval. In fact next April I'm publishing an 'end-of-the-hippies' novel." I was left with a book that cried out to be written even if nobody wanted it—a situation that seemed all too familiar.

In our search for alternative meditation techniques, one night we attended a lecture at the East-West Cultural Center in downtown Los Angeles. The star attraction was a famed Sufi mystic named Pir Zade. The moment we entered the hall on West Ninth Street, we moved into an air of reverence so thick we could feel it. The lecture room was crammed with excited middle-aged people talking about the great Sufi master.

Ten minutes after the announced starting time, the front door opened, a few advance guards passed through and then Pir Zade himself. A collective gasp greeted his arrival. "Look how he glows!" whispered a woman near us. "Yes, you can actually see his light!" another agreed.

We studied him more closely and found a slim, smiling Persian of medium height, forty-five to fifty years old, wearing a closely wound turban around his head. Though he was undoubtedly charismatic, the halo seen by others in the room somehow escaped us. When he launched into a short nuts-and-bolts dissertation on how to achieve a "healing mantle of light," we took scrupulous notes.

As with many of the Eastern-style methods, visualization was involved. Starting with the head, the meditator imagines a crown of light around it glowing brightly, and once that is all lit up, you do the same for your chest area, then the solar plexus, and finally the groin. When the four centers have been illuminated, you're supposed to hold that state as long as you can. That, said Zade, activates the "third eye" in the middle of the forehead—the pineal gland—triggering a process of bodily health, mental control, and soul growth. The third eye is the key to it all.

At home we meditated the Sufi way a few weeks and found that after a few minutes of concentration, we could feel a tickling sensation inside the middle of our foreheads, along with a definite calming effect. Our third eyes were in business! We shared with our friends the new "light meditation" we'd found. In turn we were introduced to the Suleiman's mandala—a concentric design that when stared at long enough produced a buzz in the third eye—and a variety of sound mantras.

The Beatles were pushing a tiny white-bearded guru named Maharishi Mahesh Yogi, who claimed to offer secret, individually tailored Sanskrit words that when chanted brought instant peace, power, and prosperity. When we found out their Maharishi was selling his "secret words" for a hundred dollars a pop, we put him in the same bag with Scientologists and other modern heirs of the old temple moneychangers.

That's when I decided Eastern meditation was really quasi-hypnosis, a way of escaping from unpleasant realities. Juneau quietly resumed meditating the Masters way, still hoping for psychological insights.

♦

In most lives, there comes a time when things happen so fast you get swept along and it takes years to figure out what happened. For Juneau and me, 1968 marked that time. The Vietnam War burned white hot, and for the first time since the war began, the media turned against their own government. That signaled it was safe to be against the war. When Lyndon Johnson came to Los Angeles for a gala fund raiser, ten thousand uninvited guests gathered to greet him outside the Century Plaza Hotel.

Juneau and I went early to see the show. Unlike previous demonstrations, this one had a distinctly middle-class flavor as middle-aged men in business suits and well dressed women mixed uneasily with long hairs, hippies, and blue-jeaned radicals. The minority handful of folks in our thirties age group greeted one another like long-lost relatives. Despite the occasional draft card burning and filthy speech advocates, the mood remained light and upbeat.

We kept craning our necks for a glimpse of the presidential limousine and its entourage of cabinet members, but when they didn't show, word passed through the crowd that Johnson had flown in by helicopter and been whisked inside from the hotel roof. Nerves grew frayed, more bored, though, than angry. Later that afternoon police reinforcements arrived from nowhere and began pushing the crowd back with batons.

A squad car with speakers on its roof drove onto the sidewalk, and a police captain with a mike stepped out. "This demonstration is illegal!" he bellowed. "As of fifteen minutes ago, your stated time limits have been exceeded. We ask that you now leave peaceably the way you came!" He repeated the announcement, and the crowd began to stir. A phalanx of motorcops roared into view and stopped on the plaza, revving their Harleys for emphasis. Juneau and I were about to leave when young black men with red armbands jumped out in front of us.

"You can't leave that way!" they yelled. "The pigs got the whole place sealed off!"

"How do we get out of here?" asked a man in a suit. Several family groups with baby carriages wheeled around in circles while the crowd pressed in toward the hotel.

"The only way out is around the hotel!" someone shouted.

Barring the way stood a long blue rank of policemen, batons held at the ready. The surge at our backs pushed us toward them but we resisted, unwilling to put our heads under their truncheons. Off to the right, we heard someone yell. A woman shrieked, and the crowd parted long enough for us to glimpse a blond-haired man holding his head, blood streaming between his fingers. Standing right before us, a red-headed cop about my size anxiously watched the surging mob. Seeing the situation through his eyes, outnumbered a hundred to one, I couldn't help feeling sorry for him. Suddenly, a young black man grabbed my arm and began pushing me toward the cop.

"Time for action, man!" he urged. "Go off that pig!"

The cop raised his club and waved it menacingly, moving toward me. Holding up my arm to ward off potential blows, I turned to the black instigator.

"Hey, man, why don't *you* get him if you're so gung ho?" I asked.

The youth looked startled, mumbled, and moved off to goad on someone else. Holding hands, Juneau and I pushed against the mob flow back toward Santa Monica Boulevard. We'd take our chances at being "sealed off." As we worked our way through the milling bodies, we heard the roar of motorcycles moving out and anguished shouts, screams, and cursing coming from the rear. Forging ahead until the crowd thinned, we found ourselves walking the grass lanes with a sparse handful of other escapees. The rear had not been sealed off at all. The radical tacticians had simply manufactured a "police confrontation," resulting in scores of innocent people suffering split skulls and broken bones, many injured by the frenzied mob crush.

Movement leaders called it police brutality, and the underground press played up the event as the first "pig riot." Even the *L.A. Times* reported not a single word about the black instigators stirring up all the trouble. You had to be there to know. Years later a good friend, LAPD Sergeant Cary Krebs, told us he'd been there that day as part of their Swat team. Cary was stationed in front of the hotel doors with orders to fire his weapon at anyone getting by the front cordon of officers.

Inside the doors, had the demonstrators penetrated the first two lines of defense, two FBI men with Gatling guns stood ready to mow down hundreds—a massacre that would have provided lots of martyrs for our movement manipulators to exploit. That Century City stampede underlined our growing doubts about the movement. While we hated the bureaucratic cynicism in Washington that looked on young Americans as so much jungle fodder, we had grown equally suspicious of the anti-American conspirators pulling strings behind every cause, ready to sacrifice *your* all for *their* power trip. If government could not be trusted, neither could the disloyal opposition. That was when we began to suspect our answer did not lie in plotting overthrows of the system.

Driving along the freeway one day, I was dialing around the radio when I came across a taped repeat of Roy Masters analyzing a troubled soul. The caller asked if the core of his philosophy were not based on the Judeo-Christian concept.

"Yes, it is," Masters said in his velvety East End London accent.

"If that's so, how can man get something from inside himself when he is basically evil and vicious and apart from truth?" the caller asked.

"The world is evil," he replied. "You are part of that evil until you meditate and invite the Light to guide you. That way you learn to become a good person."

"But the Bible tells us that no one is good, that we need a savior to give us the power to combat evil."

"You see? You are caught up worshiping a book instead of the Creator. There are great words of wisdom in the Bible, but it is not the fount of wisdom. It mustn't be used as a source. You must find your own source of power through meditating."

Masters went on to chastise "servants of evil" who did not want people to see the Light, modern pharisees and lawyers. He called off a list of conspirators fighting to keep his truth from people, including doctors, scientists, ministers, sociologists, and rabbis. Since I suspected lots of conspiracies myself, I found myself agreeing with him.

I began listening to his show whenever I could, and soon his philosophy became a part of my own. Closely tied to Freudian theory, it echoed the Jewish belief that a good person will be rewarded with peace and happiness. It mixed a hodgepodge of Pavlov, moral judgments, and blanket condemnation of anyone disagreeing with Masters as the final arbiter of truth. Though theoretically the Light beckoned to all, in practice it was available only to those who learned to meditate the Roy Masters way.

One Saturday afternoon, I sat down and listened to the record Juneau had bought. Master's patter was just the sort of discourse one might expect from a former hypnotist, full of suggestions and beguiling implants. His technique involves closing your eyes, fixing attention on your hands, looking out the center of your forehead with your mind's eye—the third eye—and watching your thoughts for weaknesses so you can "grow out of them" to perfection. It was the mental equivalent of patting your head while rubbing your stomach, all narrated in such sweet seductive tones it seemed totally nonthreatening. So, joining Juneau, I started doing his meditation exercise on a daily basis.

Along with meditating his way, we found ourselves becoming fans of his radio show. Not that we learned much new—he had just one theme with limited variations—but we enjoyed gloating over the way Masters argued with detractors, browbeat callers who didn't agree with him, and ridiculed other religions as "blind leaders of the blind." Over the next few months we found our views growing more and more like his—added proof we were seeing "truth" and everyone else was all wet.

◆

When Martin Luther King was murdered in Memphis, shock waves spread across the land with rioting and looting in many big-city black neighborhoods. A Socialist group called the Peace and Freedom Movement called a vigil for King outside the federal building downtown near Pershing Square. Juneau and I joined a few hundred mostly black mourners and listened to four hours of verbal rage matching our feelings. Two weeks later the Peace Action Council, an ad hoc Socialist front, called a demonstration in honor of King to "end racism and repression in America."

While we stood in front of City Hall listening to the same bitter rhetoric from the same faces, plain-clothed policemen stood on raised mounts snapping pictures of the white participants. By then we'd been to so many demonstrations and signed so many checks and petitions, we felt sure the government didn't need snapshots to know where to find us. So we smiled at the lens and held up finger V's for victory.

With King gone, we hoped for a new leader to restore the republic. Robert Kennedy filled that role for us. As much as we admired his brother John, we adored Bobby's intensity and commitment to blacks, poor people, and the war's end. When he was murdered, our hope died with him. We became bitter and cynical. Maybe the radicals were right. Maybe the whole system was just too corrupt—maybe it needed to be destroyed.

So we joined the Socialist Peace and Freedom Party and then the radical Friends of the Black Panthers. Far from being Socialists or Marxist revolutionaries, we were just a pair of disillusioned idealists desperate for something to believe in. Some of us took to the streets, others plotted crazy actions behind closed doors, a few marched around with rifles or planted bombs—most of us just went to demonstrations, gave money to action groups, shook our clenched fists, shouted, "All power to the people!" and secretly despaired.

That summer the Black Panthers dominated newscasts when Chicago police made a predawn raid on local Panther headquarters, killing two and wounding five. In early December, the LAPD went after the Los Angeles Panther chapter with hundreds of heavily armed officers. Fourteen Panthers held off the attackers for five hours while their apartment was shredded by gunfire and tear gas. Our Friends support group visited the site two days later for a grand tour. The acrid stench of gas was still potent enough to trigger tears, and as we marched through the rooms, Panther guides pointed out blood stains and a gaping hole in the ceiling where police helicopters had bombed the roof.

At a protest demonstration two days later, Juneau, I, and a few score mostly black stalwarts listened to the same predictable "rhetoric of rage" from the same movement leaders monitored by a few police squad cars. This morning one white hippy type hung around us, offering friendly remarks and handing us salted nuts.

"It just goes to show you," he commented. "It pays to have a gun. If those Panthers hadn't fired back, they'd all be dead today."

"I suppose," Juneau commented.

"These days you got to be crazy not to have a gun—a couple guns," he said. "Do you folks have any guns?"

"No, we don't believe in owning guns," I said.

The hippy shrugged. "It's your life," he said.

"Why would anyone want to attack us?" Juneau asked.

"These days? Are you kidding!" the man asked. "Look, if they can kill Kennedy and King just to get rid of them, why would they think twice about you?"

"You have a point," I said, just to put him off. "Maybe I should buy myself some weapons."

"Now you're talking sense," the man said.

He slipped away soon after that, and we forgot about the incident—until the day when we came back from work and Juneau got a call from Tina DeAngelo next door. Two men in business suits driving a dark car had been on the block. They hung around long enough to take out a camera and shoot pictures of our house from lots of angles before leaving.

"Did they say who they were?" Juneau asked.

"No—and I didn't ask them," Tina said. "Is everything okay?"

"Of course," Juneau said. "And thanks for telling us."

The moment she hung up, paranoia set in. I worked up a scenario of the FBI casing our place for a Panther-type raid. Knowing we owned no guns, they could wipe us out in seconds without risk.

"Maybe it's time to get ourselves a couple of rifles," I said grimly. "If they want to kill us, let's not go easy like German Jews to a gas oven. Let's take a couple of those —— — with us."

Hashing out the pros and cons of buying weapons and learning how to use them, we then turned to defensive measures. That weekend I crawled under the house to scout out a hiding place in the event of attack, planning to sandbag a dugout in front of a vent. We even priced bags at a lumber yard and looked at rifles in sporting goods stores. Then, like having a bucketful of ice water poured over our fevered heads, we came to our senses. Was this what life was really about? Maybe all this political stuff was a dead end. Antiwar sentiment was now so popular even Nixon was cooing like a dove and Jane Fonda came out of the woodwork from nowhere making noises like she'd been a Vietcong for years. We may have been against the war but not against the U.S.A. Before wasting our lives with sandbags and rifles battling nightmares, maybe we should find out who we were and why we were here?

◆

Now we turned to meditating with a vengeance. Three times or more a day, we sat down and practiced the Masters' routines. The more we got into it, the more attached we grew to Masters' voice on the radio. For years I'd suffered severe migraine headaches that mere aspirin could not help. Using the Masters method, when I felt one coming on, I had a way to fight back. Though the migraines didn't disappear, at least they were more endurable, and I felt more in control of my destiny.

Juneau found no such relief for her PMS and cramps. According to Masters' doctrine, it was her own fault. Illness, he taught, was the outward proof of one's inner evil. Roy claimed to have enjoyed instant healing when he fell off his motorcycle and shattered his hip, proof of his perfection. When she became right, Juneau would be healed the same way.

Before long meditation became a quick fix to relax our minds. Sitting down, we could clear our heads of worries in a matter of a minute or two, then we would ask to be shown as much of the truth as we could bear to see that day. Our yearning for truth, without our realizing it, was a call for the Holy Spirit.

The truths we expected to see were past experiences that were poisoning our lives. Instead, we became aware of what a cheat smoking cigarettes was. We smoked them to bring peace, and they really didn't deliver. Reaching for the pack every time we felt uptight, we had to go back again and again for a useless crutch. How stupid to continue! So we stopped, and were never tempted to smoke them again. Of course, we continued to use marijuana but rationalized that as being far less harmful since we smoked just one of those a day instead of the forty cigarettes we used to smoke.

One evening we attended a Roy Masters lecture at his Foundation of Human Understanding, a storefront on Western Avenue. Fifty older people sat on folding chairs before a small podium. Tables and wall racks were bulging with tracts, records and books. Our first impression was disappointment. This group looked no different from UFO and spiritualist crowds we'd seen, mostly people broken by life and afraid of death.

A fortyish nondescript man pitched the organization

and its products, then introduced Masters who bounded out from a back room grinning. Though we were predisposed to like him, his talk added little new to what we'd learned from his record and writings. His rambling discourse went on far too long, and he had an annoying habit of misquoting classics or attributing statements to the wrong sources, all done with great authority. Even during the Q-and-A period, audience questions seemed intended more to ingratiate the speaker than to challenge him. The only real sparkle came when, for no apparent reason, Masters chastised an elderly woman as "meddlesome and judgmental" for complaining about her children's neglect. But even as he criticized her, the giggle in his voice softened the edge, and she smiled her thanks. When he finished his talk, the usual postlecture klatch surrounded him so we bought a few books, chatted briefly with his aide, and left.

A month later we tried again, with much the same results. This time, after the lecture Masters left his admirers and came over to us. Up close his eyes were sparkly blue and his grin engaging.

"What did you think?" he asked me.

"Very interesting," I replied. "We're using your record and getting a lot out of it."

"Aha!" he beamed. "You have a lot to learn yet—but I have a feeling about you." He looked hard into my eyes, then turned to Juneau. "Are you meditating, too?"

"Yes," she said. "I started before he did."

"It often happens that way," he said. "Women are more sensitive and I can tell, you've had a very hard life. Would you leave your names with Jerry here? I'd like to add you to our mailing list if you don't mind."

Jerry Olsen, his right-hand man, took our address and telephone number. As we left, he called out, "Thanks for coming. Roy will be in touch!"

Realizing early on the danger of Roy's voice being a focus for anyone's meditating, even over radio, I was convinced the process should be learned through the written word to avoid any attachment to the teacher. Still, meditation was our salvation and salvation meant Masters, until it seemed clear that Roy Masters was the most exalted of all modern mystics. Every morning and evening without fail we'd do the meditation exercise. With his constant exhortations to be "patient, kind and understanding," Masters seemed nothing less than a second coming of Christ.

Even at work during the day, whenever I felt stressed or uptight I'd sneak off to the men's room, find a stall, and tune in for a ten-minute refresher session. Ever with us was his dire warning sounding in our heads—"Do not fail to meditate even a single day because the moment you do, you will fall back to your old ways!" Long-time friends stopped coming by, wearied by our relentless proselytizing. Meditation and Roy Masters became our be-all and end-all, and we gave away books and records to anyone who showed even a polite interest.

Meanwhile, I'd found the "hook" for my Haight-Ashbury book. My hero, a young college student from Seattle who drops out to "find himself," would discover a lecturer at the God's Eye Theater who speaks to his heart. The mysterious unnamed stranger, who preaches the "truth that sets you free" and gives out free instructions for a way to erase the evil effects of childhood conditioning, would be a disciple of none other than—Roy Masters.

As my book developed, it became a repository of hippy artifacts—reprints of underground cartoons, stories and poetry, photos of sixties artwork, street flyers, posters, and song lyrics. And underlying it all, the theme of a young man's search for his own soul. What had started out as a six-month paperback quickie was turning into a multiyear opus.

Inspired by the underground press, Juneau and I decided to publish *Diary of a Deaf Mute* in its original English. This was to be an act of love, making the novel available to any who might enjoy it even if it were not "commercially viable" for major publishers.

Scouting around for U.S. printers, we found them far too expensive for a limited edition of two thousand copies. So I wrote to my English publisher who recommended a Surrey printer for the job. A beautifully printed saddle-stitched paperback with cover art showing a pair of worried eyes—

courtesy of Juneau—arrived one afternoon in eight huge cardboard crates, which we stored in our garage. With lists of bookstores and distributors purchased from the trade magazine *Publishers Weekly*, we mailed out a replica of the cover plus a letter soliciting sales. That effort brought in several hundred orders, most of them from small town or university outlets.

Putting in calls to major wholesalers, I met a few buyers and placed five hundred more copies—all on speculation. I sent review copies to newspapers around the country, then another mailing to radio and TV talk shows, attracting bookings with cultural FM radio and UHF television stations in New York, New Haven, Providence, Boston, Philadelphia, Washington, D.C., and Cleveland. Squeezing appearances into ten days of cramped Greyhound bus travel, I found myself discussing the new existentialism with my reward a mention of the book and its publisher.

When I got home, individual mail orders came to our box number, encouraging me to set up a western tour. This time we booked appearances over long weekends and in odd snatches whenever we could get away from work. I'd like to report how the phone rang off the hook and we had to go back for more printings—but that's not how it was. Instead, the books moved slowly. Before long, though, we were down to our last big crate and had paid off the costs of doing it ourselves.

But the real payoff came that spring afternoon when the National Book Awards nominated *Diary* for its prestigious prize. It marked the first time a novel from a "little publisher" had been so honored, and it gave me the shot in the arm I needed to pull back my ears and settle in to finish the hippy novel.

◆

One afternoon at home, a friend called from the beach.

"Hold on," he said. "There's an old friend of yours here who'd like to say hello."

I waited until a familiar voice said, "Hello, David. This is Bob Summers. It's been a long time."

"It sure has." I wondered what he was up to. "How are you, Bob?" I asked.

"I'm having a few problems, feeling a little nervous. It's a hard life for a playwright, but I'm looking forward to setting up some good contacts in Los Angeles. I understand you really have it together now."

"Can't complain," I said.

"I'd like to get together," he said.

"Sure thing. But we're going to have to talk about what happened in Sweden, get that straightened out."

Silence at the other end. "It's warm here," he said.

"Juneau and I are meditating," I said. "Getting your mind still really helps. I think it's something you can use. If you give me your address, I'll send you instructions."

"That sounds good. But I'm in transit. I haven't got a mail drop. I'll write you when I'm settled."

He hung up. He never did write. Six months later I was reading *The Smith,* a literary magazine out of New York, and I saw in a small blackbordered insert the announcement: "Playwright Robert N. Summers Dead At 42."

Calling friends in Philadelphia, we learned Bob had hanged himself in Larry King's apartment where he was staying. Larry walked into the bedroom one afternoon and found him dangling by the neck from a light fixture. I remembered Bob's telling me how he had, as a teenager, found his own father hanging from the ceiling. The New York literary underground mourned his passing as a "great light gone forever," but we recalled the words of Exodus 20:5: "I the Lord thy God am a jealous God, visiting the iniquity of the fathers upon the children unto the third and fourth generations of them that hate me." It was a verse I'd retained from childhood, one we used to justify our faith in Freudian psychology and the conditioned responses that made people repeat the mistakes of their parents.

11

◆

The Guru

Late one weekday afternoon just before dinner the doorbell rang and Juneau answered. I was in my office writing when I heard her effusive greeting and went out to find Roy Masters waiting in the living room.

"Hello, David," he said in silky tones.

"Hi, Roy," I countered. "What a pleasant surprise. Can you stay for dinner?"

"No, I really have to run. My wife and kiddies would be upset if I didn't show up. Perhaps another time."

"Terrific."

My eyes fixed for the first time on a packet he held in the crook of his left arm. Masters explained that it was the rough draft of his monthly manuscript, sent out to all Foundation donors. He asked if I could check it out for grammar and spelling, edit in his penciled inserts, and type it out by the end of the week.

"Sure thing," I said. "You've got yourself an editor."

Suddenly, his face darkened. "I don't really need an editor. Just fix the spelling and grammar. My writing may not be elegant, but everything I write has to stay just the way it's written. You must understand that!"

"Sure, no problem," I said, taken aback by the mercurial mood change. "Strictly grammar and spelling."

He grinned and patted my shoulder tenderly. "Thanks. I knew the first time that I laid eyes on you you would have a special role to play with the foundation."

After he'd gone, we basked in the reflected glory. Masters saw something special in me and, by extension, Juneau too. That made us special, as if God Himself had graced us through His prophet. Over the following weeks Roy faithfully dropped off manuscripts and picked up my retyped corrected copies, staying long enough to ask a few challenging questions, which I answered with trembling, afraid he'd see through to my unworthy soul. When he continued to use me, I was sure I'd passed the ultimate test.

One night just before bedtime the phone rang. It was Roy, voice purring like honey.

"I'm having the 'inner sanctum' out to the house this Saturday," he explained. "I'd like you and your wife to join us for dinner, if you can."

"I'm sure we can," I shot back without even checking the calendar.

He gave me an address in Ventura Keys, a posh seaside development up the coast toward Santa Barbara, and suggested we arrive about three. The two-story house was built edging a waterway connecting to the Channel Islands harbor. Roy's wife, Ann, let us inside where a dozen adults stood around munching snacks. At the rear of the house, Roy was bellowing at five little kids playing in the backyard. The house was in bedlam, but I gazed past the turmoil to the lawn sloping down to the water. There, rigging framed against a cloudless sky, a double-masted schooner stood moored to the dock, gently rolling with the tidal swells. It was a beautiful sight for landlocked eyes.

Soon Roy came bounding over to apologize for the noise and introduce us to the gang. The mood was light, but conversation focused on Roy. The staffers traded stories of how Roy handled wicked troublemakers at the lectures or confounded angry husbands who came to the foundation ready to punch his nose for alienating their wives only to end up buying a record and becoming devoted meditators.

Just before dinnertime, Ann disappeared into the

kitchen to feed the kids. Then the rest of us formed a car caravan and drove to a nearby family restaurant where a banquet room had been set up to accommodate us. After taking his place at the head of the U-shaped double table, Roy sat us in turn according to status. Not surprisingly, Juneau and I were given the end spots of the U, farthest away from the host.

Conversation was commonplace, and the company as mentally invigorating as a Rotary parlay. When the evening ended, we thanked Roy, shook hands with his inner circle, and drove back home feeling high as kites over breaking bread with the anointed one. I continued to edit Roy's writings without pay or credit, and we meditated religiously, listened without fail to his radio shows, taped them for posterity and—of course—sent in our regular monthly offerings to advance the work.

Writing on the hippy book was nearing completion when fate stepped in to change our lives. One afternoon at work the big boss called me into a private conference with an offer he thought I couldn't refuse. Since I'd successfully arranged American distribution for Scandinavian fish canneries and architectural accessories, he knew I was the ideal person to pitch research projects to U.S. corporations. Though it would mean more travel, the fatter paycheck would more than make up for a few weekends on the road. It would also merit a change in title—how did "vice president" sound?

I could read the unbelieving shock in his eyes when I turned him down. I explained again my commitment to writing. With a book even now in progress, extra money meant less to me than extra time in front of the typewriter. Two weeks later, he buzzed me again and told me my wish had been granted. The firm was being reorganized with staff cutbacks and—taking account of my outside writing commitments—from now on I'd be on half time doing marketing reports and directing special projects. At half pay, of course.

The following week when Roy came by to drop off his manuscript, Juneau made a pot of tea as we sat chatting. Roy liked the way she made it English style, preheating the teapot before steeping.

"We really could use you down at the foundation," he said. "Bob is trying to produce the show as well as oversee printing, publicity, and everything else. It's more than he can handle, but there's no one right enough to help out. Too bad your schedule is so filled."

"Not any more," I said. "I've got half my time free now."

"I had a feeling about that," he grinned. "Can you come by the foundation tomorrow morning? I'll have Bob talk to you about arrangements."

From that day forward I joined the four other paid staffers down at the foundation, editing Roy's writings and handling publicity and promotional tours. The pay was strictly minimum wage, but the psychic reward of knowing we were spreading truth to suffering souls more than compensated for the meager biweekly checks.

Up to then Roy's radio show was carried on just the one Los Angeles station while his outside appearances were limited to lectures at a few liberal churches and rare interviews on small local television shows. Applying my book tour contacts as a base, I called around and built a national network of talk show producers who would be open to future visits from the "dynamic Roy Masters." Using his self-published book *How Your Mind Can Keep You Well* as the vehicle, I booked him on top local TV and radio shows in San Diego and Los Angeles so he could fine tune his style, make his mistakes where they'd not be so devastating, and learn how to be a guest instead of a garrulous guru.

Roy had a problem relating to hosts. He would start fights with them, try to show them up, and convert them—and so alienate their fans. But Roy insisted he made no mistakes, and the people around him supported his view that the world was against him while he was perfect in all he said and did.

His claim to perfection was the catch-22 for any sincere follower. Whereas mere mortals like ourselves regarded our spiritual growth as movement from gross error toward ever improving grace, there always remained impure thoughts and irritations to remind us we were less than divine. But Roy had no such constraints; whatever he did *had* to be right since *he* was right. So even when you saw him goof or act with feet of clay, he rationalized it away as a ploy to teach you or someone else a spiritual lesson.

Even when ardent followers charged him with being the Christ, he would smile benevolently and nod as if to say, "Only the Holy Spirit could have told you that truth." Having to stifle what my eyes were seeing and my ears were hearing produced conflict and a burning conscience, but with half my week spent away from the foundation I could regain my bearings and the pain of choking back the truth receded.

My efforts on his behalf were paying big dividends. In a four-month stretch, I'd arranged two tours back East to Boston, Providence, upstate New York, and New York City where he'd guested on ten shows in four days. I could have set up double the number but Roy hated being away from his family and loyal supporters.

The appearances generated lots of new orders for books and records and provided leverage for me to get major chains like Doubleday's, Brentanos, and Pickwick's to stock his book. At the same time I'd sent query letters to major New York publishers, alerting them to his media schedule and acting as agent for Roy's book. Several asked for reading copies as a result, and one—a Simon and Schuster editor—even telephoned to underline his interest.

A few weeks later the editor called back to make a publishing offer. At that point Roy and Bob took over the negotiations and came out with a miserable contract. What hurt most was their denying I had had anything to do with the sale. Nursing my bruised ego, I consoled myself with the thought I was growing more mature by not sharing in the glory.

Among Masters' more unsavory teachings was his doctrine on women. Men, he preached, were led by sexual lust for women. That was how evil and temptation, which always came through the woman, were able to enter man's body. It was the woman, he always reminded us, that Satan used to tempt poor Adam from his pristine innocence. As a male supremacist who believed woman's place was in the home, barefoot and pregnant, he constantly griped about his own wife who he believed was not meditating right since she did not treat him as reverently as he thought she should.

One day Roy began complaining about "poor Irving Goode" and how he was getting "caught up" with the foundation. Irving, a man in his midfifties, was an early follower, volunteer, and devotee. His attachment to Roy was so intense his wife threw him out of the house. So he bought a boat and lived on it down at Marina Del Rey, spending most of his time hanging out at the foundation where he helped sell materials, greeted visitors and enjoyed insider status. When an intruder broke in one night and stole some office machines, Irving offered to sleep on a broken-down cot in the back room. But all his efforts to ingratiate himself failed. When he developed jaw cancer that made him physically repugnant, condemnation quickly followed since Roy taught that cancer was a vile disease attacking only the most wicked of people—human vampires who live off the life energies of others.

"Irving's not right," Roy groused to whoever was around. "He's caught up with me, he needs to get away for his own good."

When Irving didn't take the hint to leave, Roy told Bob to remove his cot and collect his key. Irving responded by taking his sleeping bag to the floor, refused to hand over the key, and Bob had the unhappy task of ordering him out. Irving bellowed like a wounded elephant, cursed his leader, and vowed to come back to shoot first Roy, then Bob. The outburst upset everyone, particularly Bob and Roy who feared his pistol more than his mouth.

Roy began on-air diatribes about the deterioration of America. Things were getting so bad, he said, with rebels out of control, the only sensible response for good people was to make sure they and their families survived the harsh times. That meant freeze-dried foods, survival packs, isolated hideaways and—most crucially—rifles, guns, and ammunition. Outside the control booth, there was a feverish rush to carry out the master's plan. Aides were sent on shopping trips, returning with bulk buys of restaurant-sized canned goods, sacks of barley, rice, and grains, and other supplies that were heaped into a room and sold to staffers, families, and friends of the foundation. Roy, Bob and other insiders stocked their homes and armed themselves to the teeth.

I was the only holdout. Interpreting my unwillingness to buy weapons as a criticism of themselves, the others pressured me to follow suit. One afternoon Roy came into my office urging me to do everything necessary to protect my family.

"I went through this once before, Roy," I told him. "A year ago I was sure that the CIA would shoot up my house, that I needed guns, sandbags, the whole thing. Juneau and I decided against the guns then and have no reason to change our minds."

As the weeks went by and Irving never put in his appearance as a revengeful sniper, talk of armed conflict gradually subsided. But Roy bought a farm in Ojai, a getaway where he held weekend retreats at $250 a head. During the summer months, he promoted daylong sailing trips on his sloop for $125 where up to twenty devotees could learn at the master's feet and catch a few mackerel in the bargain.

As bookkeeper, Russ told me about strange money handling during evening lectures. Daily, Russ opened the mail, counted the offerings, and entered them in the ledger, but at the lectures Ann Masters eagerly grabbed the paper shopping bag full of cash. The reason—that "the Foundation was in a high-crime area and it would be safer with them at home than in the building"—had a phony ring, since there was a huge safe in the back of the building. But no amount of reasoning prevailed. Roy and Ann always took the lecture money home with them and Russ, just a hired hand, had to go along with the questionable practice. "Roy had hang-ups dealing with money," Russ noted.

Yet, despite clear signs that our "perfect master" was all too humanly imperfect, he exercised a hypnotic effect on all those he'd chosen as his employees. During an earlier career running a hypnosis institute, he learned how to recognize people who would respond to his suggestions. Evidently, there is a weakness in our makeup that makes us vulnerable to hero worship. He knew that the record hooked the meditators to his voice, and he often told listeners to practice with the record again—they needed "reinforcement." At the same time he warned them, "Don't get caught up with me," so they would blame their guru worship on themselves.

He constantly played to our religious bent, our fear of God and Christ. When opportunities arose, he seemed to subtly inject the idea that he, Masters, was an incarnated Master, in fact, the greatest Master of them all—the Christ.

For two years I choked back doubts and labored heart and soul to advance the great truth of his meditation—the long lost and rediscovered "key to the kingdom," mentioned by Jesus in Matthew 16:19. I continued promoting Masters for talk shows, setting up guest shots with Mike Douglas and Tom Snyder, got Fawcett paperbacks to put out his book, and promoted enough demand in other cities to get his radio call-in program aired in Boston, San Francisco, and Seattle.

All of us underlings lived off our leader's praises and smiles. When instead we were targets of his frowns or whining complaints, it would create heartaches lasting into sleepless nights. When the stress got unbearable, I'd seek relief by meditating. When my peace finally came, there came with it the knowledge that things were not right with the foundation and I had to leave.

That was when, uncannily, the phone would ring. On the other end was Masters with some trivial request to justify calling at the strange hour. His soothing tone and heady praise soon dissolved any urge to quit. This sequence of emotional misery triggering a call from Masters became so predictable I took pride in "prophesying" to Juneau that it was Roy calling before I ever picked up the phone to confirm it. Roy had a supernormal sense of when I had reached my emotional limit and just when to bring me back in line. So, forgetting the former pain, I'd go back to work full of renewed devotion.

At this point he began stressing the mystical need to be "born again." According to Roy's version of rebirth, when anyone meditated the right way in the right spirit, that weakened the hold of evil spirits within. Soon, one day, the Light would appear to take over the individual's life. That was the meditator's moment of truth. Either he would surrender to the Light, who would take over his life in a new and miraculous way—or he would deny the Light and be guilty of the unforgivable sin, assuring an eternity in hell. It was a terrifying scenario, and I prayed that when my moment came, I would not deny that Light.

I found a way to glorify Roy Masters and get wider distribution for his meditation. My in-progress novel had a place near the end where the young hero, having learned and now using the "key of David" meditation, is told by his teacher to mimeograph the instructions and give them freely to all who will receive. So I had life imitate fiction by writing my own version of the meditation technology, toning down the hypnotic content, and stressing "centering" with the right attitude—yearning with all one's heart to have the truth revealed. I called the two-page primer "Getting Free of Conditioning." The last page of the book carried a full-blown pitch for Roy Masters and the foundation, including its address and phone number.

The novel, originally titled *Summer of Love,* was finally published by Ashley Books in late 1972. When their editor asked for a flashier alternative to *Summer of Love* in line with the longer titles of the seventies, we'd substituted *The Prodigal Pilgrim's Great Golden Gate Odyssey.* The day our complimentary copies arrived, there to surprise us was a totally new—and draggy—title, *The Spieler for the Holy Spirit.*

Swallowing our disappointment, we did the best we could to promote it. That proved to be some kind of trick, since it got not a single review anywhere. We'd never heard of such a total blackout, particularly when the author was last year's National Book Award nominee. Attributing review neglect to hatred of hippies and antiwar politics helped soothe our egoes but not our hopes of wider success. Still, the book did get into bookshops and gave me a chance to travel around plugging meditation on TV and radio shows.

During one television appearance in Cleveland, I ran into folk singer Phil Ochs on the set. We'd met at some of the movement actions years before. Now Phil was launching a "come back," hoping to recapture those special times that were the sixties. I went on first, as Phil sat below watching. After a lively ten-minute session of promoting meditation, along with the book, I came off the interview and Phil grabbed my elbow.

"Hey, man, I got to talk to you," he said earnestly. We went behind a curtain, and he looked deep into my eyes, as if searching my soul.

"Why aren't you out fighting our fight any more?" he asked. "The people need us, they need our fire, our brains—this meditation does nothing but turn you off, man. It's a real downer. Please, David, come back to the real world."

I felt sorry for Phil, moved by his desperation—but revolutionary anger was no longer in my heart. "Why don't you try meditation?" I asked. "You know as well as I do that the movement's dead."

I left him shaking his head, lost and bewildered. Two years later, Phil would end his suffering by hanging himself in his sister's house.

The book tour paid off, as Ashley eventually sold out its eight-thousand-copy first printing, mostly through word-of-mouth mail orders, and I had a remarkable experience on San Francisco's KGO radio with a tryout host named Doug Cornet.

During our morning session, we discussed how we all get trapped into childhood personality hang-ups by Pavlovian "conditioning." After a score of listener call-ins, where I applied my own version of instant psychoanalysis, I offered to send anyone who wrote me a free instruction sheet for "Getting Free of Conditioning." Giving my home address, I went to my next appearance with no great expectations. Normally a radio appearance would bring in five, a dozen, or at best twenty requests. This time, though, it was a case of Peter putting his nets out at the right time. Two days after coming back home, Juneau called me at the foundation.

"David, you won't believe this!" she said. "The mailman just dropped off a big canvas bag filled with letters!"

I couldn't wait to get home. We spent the whole evening just sorting through hundreds of letters and cards. Another bagload came in, and by the time the deluge ended a week later, we'd received over 1,200 requests! To put it in perspective, a top national show like Johnny Carson's or Donahue's will describe a guest appearance pulling 200 letters as a "flood of mail." For a local radio show, it was absolutely unprecedented. It took us three weeks working evenings and weekends to get instruction sheets and notes out to those who'd asked for them.

At the foundation, Roy asked for the first time how the book was going. I'd given him a complimentary copy which he'd never commented on. When I told him what was happening with it, he admitted he'd only read part of it. But he had seen my ad for himself, and that impressed him.

"I'd like you to come on my show and tell your story to our listeners," he said. "You have something very important to say to young people."

We set up a date for the following week. Meanwhile Bob McQuain was under fire for "not being quite right," and I felt secretly pleased to see someone other than myself on the critical list. The rest of the week passed quietly. Friday evening I felt strangely jittery and couldn't get to sleep. Thinking the house was wired with "vibrations," I went out to the guest cottage across the back yard and soon fell into a deep sleep.

Suddenly, I saw a light flash into the darkness and a blue-white brilliance loomed closer and closer until at last it dominated my vision. There was a face inside the great glow, a face not unlike Roy Masters'. Instinctively, I knew this was the Light, coming to claim me at my moment of truth. There was no time to think of what to do—I reacted instantly. Covering my eyes with my arms, I shouted "No!" as my being decided the matter. The Light vanished, and I sat up in bed trembling. It took me two hours to get back to sleep, troubled that maybe I'd decided my fate for all eternity.

Most good tidings seem to come by telephone. That Friday I got a call from Sy Paget, managing editor for Ashley, that raised our spirits sky high.

"Just got a call from Columbia University," he said matter-of-factly. "Your book has been nominated for the Pulitzer Prize in letters, and they need to know your birth date, where you were born, and your early schooling. We've given them all the rest out of your bio."

That night we celebrated by eating out at the Malibu Sea Lion. The nomination made four years of work on a book no one seemed to want worthwhile and helped us believe God was with us.

The day came when I was to go on Roy's show. When Bob told me Roy had scheduled another guest, I just assumed he'd forgotten his invitation and I chose to do the same. That afternoon he came looking for me.

"Why didn't you come in to talk about your book?" he asked.

"I thought you'd forgotten," I replied. "You had the fellow from the record company scheduled."

"I don't forget anything," he said. "I'm beyond that." He giggled, then grinned. "You're going on tomorrow. Make sure you're in the studio ten minutes before I go on."

The next day I pored through my notes, then went to the back room where the broadcast originated, sat down and waited. Roy arrived just before air time, waved at me, and slipped on his earphones. As he answered callers, he looked my way, locked eyes with mine, grinned at me, and used my nodding and encouragement for strength.

The time clicked off. The first hour passed, then half the second hour. When just twenty minutes remained, I realized he was not going to introduce me. My first instinct was to walk out and avoid confrontation, then I was moved to stay right there. When he said good-bye to his last caller and gave his sign-off pitch, he threw down the phones and let out a blast of air.

"Phew!" he said. "It was a pretty good program, don't you think?"

I didn't answer. He grinned and stood up to leave.

"Hold on, Roy," I said, controlled by an inner calm.

"Yes?"

"Why did you do that to me?"

"Do what? What are you taking about?"

"You made a point of asking me on your show," I said. "And I sat there for two hours like an idiot."

"Oh," he said. "Did I do that? I forgot."

"That won't do," I said. "You told me yourself you never forget. So what you did was a consciously cruel act. It was wrong, you hurt me, and now you've got to deal with it."

He stared at me a long time, probing for weakness. Not finding what he was looking for, at last his shoulders slumped and a weak grin came on his lips.

"I guess you've won this time," he said.

"I've what?" I couldn't believe my ears. Won? Won what? Then it hit me. Roy saw every personal encounter as a competition with a winner and a loser. The whole notion of sacrificial Christian love was foreign to him. Any remaining respect vanished, leaving only mild loyalty for his launching me on a daily routine that eventually led me to the Holy Spirit.

A week later Roy called me into his office where administrator Arlen Hahn and Bob McQuain sat waiting.

"We've just had a meeting, David," he said. "Finances are down, and Bob has had to make some tough decisions. Isn't that right, Bob?"

McQuain turned red. "Yes, we have to double up on our coverage. We have a volunteer to edit the monthly manuscript, and I'll be taking over publishing, promotion, and bookstores. So it looks like . . . uh . . ."

"My job's been eliminated," I finished.

"That's the way it looks," Roy said. "We appreciate your help and expect to call on you from time to time if that's okay."

"Since this is good-bye time, let's make it official," I said. "I have to tell you, Roy, in all love that you're a greedy man.

You have a problem with money, with sharing and paying people who work for you. Far worse, though, is your claim of being perfect because it leads people astray. There's only one Number One and that's God. You not only hurt yourself with that perfection nonsense, you hurt your family and followers. Maybe you'd better rethink that perfection business."

"How dare you!" Roy cried. "I insist you apologize at once, or I never want you to set foot in here again!"

I shrugged. "Then I guess you'll just have to muddle along without me."

Back at my desk I packed my belongings into my case, said good-bye to Russ at the front desk, and walked out of the foundation for the very last time. There was something very clean and right about it. I never did receive my last paycheck, and I can only hope Roy donated it to a worthy charity.

As for me, I was free to seek the real truth. A smutty gray blob along with a weakness for phony gurus had finally and forever lifted off my soul.

12

Coming Home

hange was in the air. The Vietnam War ended as China entered a new era of friendship with America, and what little honor remained with the Nixon administration was being systematically shredded in the Senate's Watergate hearings.

Along with history, our own lives entered a new phase. Leaving the foundation meant I had a half week free time, which I determined not to hire out to a new employer. Up to now I'd avoided journalism like the plague, convinced only fiction and poetry were worthy of a wordsmith's labors. My father's unhappy experience reporting for the Yiddish newspaper *Forward* had soured his spirit for journalism, a legacy he'd imparted to me.

But after two decades of supporting my writing with another job, heartened by Marquis adding my bio to *Who's Who in America,* I decided to try my hand as a free-lance magazine writer. That meant starting from scratch because all my previous writing credits in this country involved novels and short stories. So by trial and many errors, I learned the art of writing query letters, where the free-lancer must sell himself and his article in two or three tantalizing paragraphs. It soon became clear editors were more impressed with my research background than the fact I wrote novels, even ones nominated for top literary awards.

After many months of struggle, I began getting assignments—a few from top national magazines, others from less prestigious publications, none of them big spenders. Contrary to popular belief, I found that even giants like *TV Guide* pay their writers meagerly, a six-hundred-dollar first-sale fee for a heavily researched twelve-hundred-word article. That meant I had to write fast and keep my query ideas flooding the market. As I learned the free-lancing ropes and developed contacts with editors, we learned as a family how to get by on little.

Spiritually, Juneau and I entered a new, surprising phase. Drawn like magnets to the Bible, we spent our free time studying the Word or reading aloud to each other and discussing what we didn't understand. Though continuing to meditate every morning, it was more a daily dedication to truth and God's will than the do-it-yourself salvation taught by Roy Masters. The more we got into the Bible, the more convinced we were of its truth. Most of our study centered on the Psalms, the Prophets, and the Gospels. Though attracted to the portrait of Jesus, we regarded Him as an exalted teacher and prophet but certainly not the Son of God.

One afternoon as Juneau walked through the living room, she took note of the swelling of pride she got from gazing at her paintings on the wall. Just a few months ago she'd had a showing on a Los Angeles television show, and by now the ego glow had extended to the way she had decorated the house. Suddenly she was struck by a verse from Exodus 20—"You shall have no other gods before Me"—the very first commandment.

A sense of sin overwhelmed her. Feeling absolutely devastated with shame over her house pride and artwork, she stripped the walls of every picture and stored them in the garage, faces to the wall. Then she took down her sculpture and decorations, packed them in boxes, and stashed them away. She remembers her feelings . . .

> *I could no longer even arrange my home in a*
> *way that encouraged my feelings of pride. By not*
> *fussing over the way it looked and letting it get a*

*little messy, I began to feel neutral about the place.
It became just a house where we lived. There was
no great decision to make. I just did it. I had to do
it.*

*David was very understanding. He knew I was
going through something, and if we had no art on
the walls or the house looked drab or the bed wasn't
made, that was just the way it was. The Holy Spirit
was moving in our house.*

*Several weeks later I began to feel guilty and
then very sad about the way I presented food. Again
it had to do with pride and, I believe, temptation.
Wasn't I asking each day, "Lead us not into temptation"? And yet my lavish preparations were tempting
us both to eat more than we needed. At the time I
didn't understand that, only that I felt guilty about
cooking. I'd been a good cook, regularly baking
health breads and cookies from my own recipes,
preparing exotic sauces and taking several hours to
fix the evening meal for just two of us. So I stopped
cooking anything I could be proud of.*

*Every night I served TV dinners, toast from
store bread, and ready-to-eat dishes. And I never
went back to cooking so elaborately again. Though I
returned to home preparation three months later, I
served mostly simple meals with short preparation
times. At the same time I began a study of nutrition,
learning how vitamins, minerals, and additives
affected health.*

*During this period, I took off my diamond ring
and put it away, along with other pieces of jewelry.
Then I packed up the sterling silver serving pieces
and put them in storage. My feeling was that if I got
rid of all the really nice things I owned, it would be
fine with me. After awhile I was shown that I was
trying to do penance, sacrificing my jewelry and
silver for the sin of pride I felt in my house. By
showing "humility" through self-mortification, I was
trying to appease God. He showed me it was my*

*relationship with all these things that was at fault,
not the things themselves. When I rejected them, that
showed me how much control they had over me.
These material things had no real power in themselves. It was the way I felt about them that was
wrong.*

*I recalled a visit to Father Divine's mission in
Philadelphia. Because Divine taught that sex was
sinful, he separated the men from the women,
husbands from their wives. Males sat on one side
of the church, females on the other. Many of his
followers lived communally in large hotels owned by
the church, and one complete floor housed only
women, another only men. Mealtime they sat at
different tables. It was a futile attempt by man to
control virtue. Instead of allowing the Holy Spirit to
preside over a right relationship between the sexes,
Divine set up rigid rules to combat sinful conduct.
His efforts proved no more successful than my own.*

*So I determined not to try to solve my pride
problem by banishing my possessions. Instead, I
would watch my attitude. In time I was able to bring
everything back inside the house. But I never again
allowed them to have the same meaning. My own
worth had nothing more to do with what I owned
or didn't own, what I wore or didn't wear, how my
house was decorated, or even the talents God had
given me. I had learned the meaning of worshiping
false gods.*

One day another strange thing happened. After reading
the Ten Commandments one Friday night, I decided we
should observe the Sabbath day and keep it holy. Overnight,
we became God-fearing, Bible-believing Jews.

Though Juneau didn't go so far as keeping a kosher
kitchen, each Friday she cleaned the house to prepare for the
Sabbath. We lit candles to remind us of the sanctity of the
day. Then on Saturday, after a special breakfast of pastry or
cake, we would spend the morning reading the Bible and

meditating on its meaning. Afternoons we'd drive to the beach or countryside, enjoy natural settings, then eat out and read the Bible again. The Sabbath discipline helped us grow in faith and understanding of God's written revelations to man, but we were never moved to attend a synagogue.

That's easy to understand since I'd grown up in an orthodox Jewish congregation and knew God was not to be found there. He was crowded out by rabbis and empty rituals. But every Saturday in our house, with our Bibles open and hearts prepared, we worshiped the Father, learned from His Word, understood Him through fear, and knew the comfort of His protective wings.

But the times really were a'changing, and so was our neighborhood in Encino. Our beautiful blue-eyed niece Tenley, who had just turned sixteen, came to visit us from Seattle. One afternoon she returned from a walk in nearby Balboa Park with her blouse ripped, bruises on her arm, and tears in her eyes. In broad daylight, two young hoodlums grabbed her and tried to drag her behind some bushes. But she managed to break loose and run home. When I called the police to report the incident, the sergeant said molestation and thuggery had become commonplace in the park.

One afternoon a few weeks later, Juneau and I were walking our dogs in that park when we saw the dogcatchers lurking a half-mile away at the other end. We snapped the leashes on the dogs, and by the time the men drove up in their truck, we were on our way home. The two uniformed officers jumped out and barred our way.

"You just broke the leash law," the senior man said. "We're going to write you up for citations."

"Our dogs are on leashes," I said. "You can't give us tickets for what you think you saw."

"Just watch me. Let me see some identification."

"I don't have any," I said truthfully. "We live just around the corner and are not in the habit of carrying identity cards."

"Come on. Don't give us that," his partner sneered. "Let's see your driver's license."

"We don't have it with us," Juneau said.

One officer grabbed our dogs and threw them into the wagon; the other seized Juneau's arm.

"You're under arrest if you can't show any I.D.," he growled.

From there, things deteriorated rapidly. Juneau demanded the release of our dogs, and one officer, feeling challenged, grabbed her shoulders. Soon they were both rolling on the grass, and as he tried to handcuff her, muscling her shoulders against the ground, I grabbed him and threw him sprawling. A crowd gathered to watch, and one fellow, upset by the odds, joined us against the dogcatchers.

The fight raged for ten minutes until an LAPD squad car pulled over, and real cops took control with consummate professionalism. After spending an hour at the station house, where we told our story to a sympathetic sergeant, we were released pending a magistrate's hearing.

We agreed the time had come to move on. When Juneau's mom came to visit, the two looked for wide open spaces where discouraging words were seldom heard. Soon they found a mountain valley called Agoura, where working ranches, cowboys, and dusty cafes blended into a few dispersed housing tracts. When they took me there to show off a lot, I gazed out at a strip of bald mountainside where even tumbleweeds feared to grow.

"Looks a little forbidding, don't you think?" I said.

"You have to use your imagination," Juneau enthused. "Once we get the fruit trees and shrubs in, you'll think it's Eden."

With the memory of the near rape and the officer mugging in Balboa Park still fresh in our minds, even a desert campsite seemed attractive. So we bought a large country lot and a forty-foot mobile home to live in, then looked for a dream design. Architect-built houses proved to be out of our price range, and the modular models we could afford had no appeal. That's when we read a classified ad headed "Houses to Move" offering to sell and truck to your lot fine houses condemned by freeway construction or commercial rezoning.

The man gave us a list of addresses, and we spent a few weekends checking them out. Then we saw our dream house, a New England charmer with a big bay window. It took less than a half-hour to cut a deal and sign the papers. The house arrived at 4:00 A.M. on a Wednesday, sawed apart and carried in by three huge tractor trucks.

Over the next year we hassled with carpenters, electricians, plumbers, masons, and carpetlayers, cajoling this one, yelling at the other, pleading with a third until the magical day they left us alone and we moved in. The change in lifestyle coincided with career moves as I started covering politics for *Family Weekly* during the 1976 election cycle.

One evening we were watching TV's local odd couple—comic Mort Sahl and veteran newscaster George Putnam—who cohosted a show called "Both Sides Now." Their guest that night was a soft-spoken political consultant named Hal Evry, who masterminded campaigns for Governor George C. Wallace of Alabama and scores of other politicians. Evry was so outspoken and outrageous in his Machiavellian analyses of how elections are won and lost that I made a note to interview him. Two weeks later I sat in his office and so began my education in the *realpolitik* of American society.

Through Evry we met a cast of unforgettable characters like Charles Wood of Dothan, Alabama, who owns a bunch of TV stations and ran for lieutenant governor of his state only to lose because he refused to "buy the black vote." At first I was skeptical, but Wood soon provided so much documentation and so many eyewitnesses—many of them courageous blacks putting their lives on the line to serve the truth—that I was forced to write an inflammatory piece titled "Buying Blacks in Alabama." The article caused a stir down South and brought some threatening phone calls.

A series of other eye-opening if not so shocking articles helped establish my by-line as a political and investigative writer. As a result, radio and TV producers began calling for guest shots promoting my magazine stories, and we got to know lots of people in broadcasting and show business. I was even hired to moderate a Metromedia TV show called "AdLib," where feminists faced off against traditionalists and angry old male chauvinists. As confrontational television, the show featured lots of flying fur, raised hackles, and enjoyed healthy ratings.

One afternoon when I entered the Sunset Boulevard studio for a taping, my producer handed me a poop sheet on the day's show. It was the closest thing they had to "research," showing who was scheduled to appear and their career claims to fame. That day's guest list included two militant women's libbers, a professorial sociologist from UCLA, and an unnamed "fundamentalist preacher" who would serve as the panel's male chauvinist. I spent the next ten minutes familiarizing myself with my guests' names and credits, and as they arrived, my producer introduced us. Soon the only one missing was the preacher, with air time just three minutes away.

Then he walked in, a cocky grin on his face. It was Roy Masters! When he spotted me, his mouth came open and he pointed at me.

"What . . . what are you doing here?" he asked.

"I moderate this show," I replied.

"You do!" He was so nonplussed he fell silent for a full twenty seconds while the producer sat him down and wired him for sound.

"One minute!" an assistant called.

I used the time to go back over my notes, making sure I had the right names and professional data matched to the right faces. As I concentrated, I became aware of Masters leaning toward me two chairs away.

"You're going to forget!" he hissed. "You will confuse every name, every face, every fact!" the ex-hypnotist commanded. "You will forget everything you ever knew!"

I shook my head and wondered how I could ever have respected, let alone been a follower of, such a man. Tuning in, I prayed for God's help just as the producer dropped his arm, the camera lights blinked red, and the studio sign flashed Quiet on Air. Looking into the lens, I launched into my introductions and set up the afternoon's discussion without stammering, groping for words, or glancing even once at the notes on my lap. It was one of the best shows I'd ever done, despite the fact our resident male chauvinist was so irrational he made a travesty of his arguments. The moment the taping ended, Masters went to the producer to ask when the show would air, then slinked out without a word to me. As a master hypnotist, he'd proven just as effective as he was "perfect."

After my two-part expose of the Nielsen ratings in *TV Guide* sparked industry-wide furor and a Ford Foundation study, Hollywood bureau head Dwight Whitney asked me to lunch at the Century Plaza Hotel. We had no sooner ordered our tomato juices when he got down to business.

"We'd like you to join our staff," he said. "Everyone is impressed with your work, and the big boss, Merrill Panitt, thinks you'd give us another dimension in reporting."

The idea of moving back into office drudgery and corporate politics triggered an involuntary shudder.

"Thanks for the vote of confidence," I replied. "I'm flattered. I love working for you, but I'll have to say no. As a reporter, I need to have some distance from my editors as well as my sources. So I think it'll work better if I stay freelance."

It would be a whole year before I wrote for *TV Guide* again. I found out the hard way they don't like their writers to say no to anything, particularly an invitation to join the family.

Sometimes for amusement we tuned in briefly to one or another TV evangelist. We responded to the seriousness with which they treated God, but we were totally turned off when they preached that Jesus was the only way to the Father. We were certain God heard the voices and prayers of sincere believers, without any go-betweens.

We had another problem with television evangelists—their incessant preoccupation with money. It seemed that every five minutes of preaching was followed by ten where they begged, pleaded, and plugged for donations, offerings, tithes, book sales, trinkets, cassettes, and holy splinters. The temple moneychangers were pikers compared to some of these well-known men of the cloth, who shamelessly play on viewers' weaknesses and guilts.

When a Canadian magazine assigned a picture story about the big money being made on the "Jesus circuit," we jumped at the chance to dramatize abuses. Over the next six weeks I interviewed ministers, singers, and authors as Juneau took photos of some big shakers in Christian circles—Wayne Coombs who runs the largest Christian talent agency, Billy Ray Hearn of Sparrow Records, Andrae Crouch, and The Disciples.

One surprise was finding an old antiwar comrade now in born-again ranks. The last time I saw Barry "Eve of Destruction" McGuire was at a protest rally in Griffith Park where he was being carried out to a paddy wagon. Now ten years later he was cutting records for Sparrow to glorify Jesus Christ, and his whole attitude had changed. He was living in a Seattle suburb, far from the golden glitter of Sunset Strip, and raising a family. Clearly, Barry had found something that worked for him, and I was glad to see that he had. As for me, I needed no go-between.

Though meeting evangelicals toned down our resentments, we felt threatened by what we saw as the "ominous message" they were selling along with the music and the oratory. "This message," I wrote, "that only Jesus can save, is a credo that promotes contempt for the beliefs of other religions, denominations, agnostics, and unbelievers."

Oddly, even as our political involvements gave way to religion, I was becoming better known as a political analyst. One day my agent, Jane Jordan Browne, called with an offer I wouldn't refuse. Harcourt Brace Jovanovich wanted to sign up a book about the big-time campaign masterminds who call the shots for all the major candidates, from congressmen to presidents. Without our knowing it, this was the turn in our sunshine road that would lead us all the way home.

It was fall 1978. Already the cast of characters vying for who would be our next president was in place and running. Over the next two and a half years Juneau and I would travel around interviewing candidates, political propagandists, pollsters, and the reclusive backroom strategists who, like field generals at war, plot the attacks, defenses, and media moves constituting modern American elections. The resulting book was called *The New Kingmakers* and solidified my reputation as a political analyst.

The book sold through three printings, got rave reviews in the *Christian Science Monitor* and *New York Daily News,* was savagely attacked by David Broder in a long *Washington Post* article, was syndicated nationally by the *New York Times,* was published in French, and was adopted as a required text by the political science graduate schools at major universities. In brief, it put me on the political map.

Heady with the attention, we decided to cash in on the notoriety by publishing a newsletter. After a six-month set-up phase, we printed a prototype sixteen-page monthly called *Inside Campaigning,* reporting on the latest campaign trends and strategies. Our sources were many of the same kingmakers we'd used as sources in the book—Matt Reese who worked both John and Bobby Kennedy's campaigns; Bob Goodman, media expert for George Bush; Cliff White, senior adviser to Ronald Reagan in 1980 and 1984; Dr. Walter De Vries, pollster for the Democratic national committee; Lance Tarrance, pollster for the Republicans; Stuart Spencer, strategist for Nelson Rockefeller, Ronald Reagan, and Gerald Ford; and Hal Evry who handled Winthrop Rockefeller and George C. Wallace—plus a slew of local professionals around the country.

Certain of big money, we bought computer equipment, ran expensive mailings, and started publishing the beginning of 1983. We had 160 subscribers, not nearly enough to make it pay, but a good start—so we thought. Among those first signups were the White House, Democratic and Republican national committees, big-name U.S. senators and representatives, the *New York* and *Los Angeles Times,* other big-city newspapers, TV network news bureaus, labor unions, political action committee (PAC) analysts, and other political professionals. It was only a matter of time, we thought, before the "big payoff." So we labored long and hard hours through the 1984 presidential cycle, reporting all the inside news and trends that became headlines a month or two later.

All the pros knew, used, and photocopied issues of *Inside Campaigning*. Calls came in from Tom Hayden's aide, complaining of short items we'd run about Jane Fonda. Others wrote protesting faulty information, real or imagined. Almost never did it turn out to be a paid subscriber. By the time Reagan won re-election to his second term, we had added only another twenty-six subscriptions despite being called an "indispensable tool" by the White House's communications director. Another six months more of such "success" would have meant losing our house. As it was, when we called it quits, we had run up a substantial five-figure debt, had lapsed all our magazine and book contacts, and seemed to be at an absolute dead end.

Paradoxically, it turned out to be a new, life-changing, final fork on our homecoming sunshine road.

13

A New Beginning

During the spring of 1984, while the primaries were in full swing, I found myself turning to chemical help nearly every day. Though I never worked high, I found myself champing at the bit for five o'clock to come around so I could scoot out to the mobile home, roll a joint, and turn on. For a few short hours my troubles melted under pot smoke, and when the buzz weakened, I'd go smoke again until bedtime when I could escape in sleep.

That was when the Spirit of Truth spoke to my heart and told me I was addicted. In the past I'd always felt justified smoking grass, believing I could take it or leave it as I pleased. Addicts, I knew, were those who couldn't say no. Weren't there plenty of days I never even thought of marijuana? Maybe not plenty, but certainly some—and those one or two days off gave me the excuse I wanted to keep the habit going. Now, though, there was no denying it. I was hooked, my mind was foggy most of the time, and with the latest research showing how marijuana smoke was fifty times more cancer causing than tobacco, it surely was time to quit. Easy enough. What I'd done with cigarettes, I could do now with pot. I'd just pray with a sincere heart, ask God to free me, and that would be it.

It was Easter week. After a hard day's work with frustrations piling in one after the other, I sat down, crossed my fingers, and began to pray.

"God, You know what's in my heart now," I told Him. "I realize I'm chained to marijuana, a slavery as real as links and locks. Please, Lord Jehovah, take this affliction from me, just as You've delivered me from cigarettes and other miseries before."

Sitting quietly in the waning hours of the day, I waited for God's answer to my prayer. At other times after such entreaties He'd filled my heart with a sweet healing that brought joy, and I knew at those times He was granting my request. Today, though, I felt no such healing balm. Instead, a still small voice spoke to my mind's ear . . .

"Ask Jesus," He said.

I couldn't believe it! Ask Jesus? I could never do that. I was humiliated by the inference. Wasn't I good enough for my Creator's personal attention? Did I need a high priest to carry my requests to Him like a middle-management hack going through channels? As a hardhearted egotist who'd always taken pride in my own strength and self-sufficiency, I couldn't deal with the fact that the number one slot in heaven had already been allotted.

But it was more than just an ego hassle. I was a Jew. I knew what it would mean if Jesus actually healed me. It was more than I could handle. Shaking off His suggestion, I lit a joint and escaped into grass. The next afternoon, though, when the marijuana demon acted up, I prayed again. Again, I got the answer I didn't want.

"Ask Jesus," He said more clearly.

Instead I gritted my teeth, went out, and smoked a double portion of pot. But the Spirit was working mightily in my life, and I slept poorly that night, despite going to bed groggy. The next day I'd have to do as I was being told.

When the word came to me a third time, I clasped my hands and prayed: "Jesus, if You are who Scripture says You are, please heal me of this marijuana curse. I ask this with a sincere heart. I ask this in truth and will serve the truth if You do this."

That was the whole prayer, lasting only a few seconds. Yet the moment I finished praying, a great weight lifted off my heart and shoulders. My head grew clear and calm. In my heart of hearts, I knew it was done. Still, I was unwilling to believe it could be that simple. Telling myself I couldn't be sure I wouldn't go back tomorrow or the next day, I held off giving thanks to the One who had rescued me.

Underlying my reluctance was an ancient terror. Though I was a Jew who didn't belong to a synagogue, I did belong to a people. I belonged to a family, a tradition, and a national identity. I was born a Jew, I would die a Jew, and I would live the rest of my life as a Jew. A media consultant friend, Eli Bleich, once told me that as a Jew growing up in New York, he learned there were two things he could never do—root for the Yankees or vote Republican. He could have added a third, and much bigger, prohibition—against Jesus as Messiah and Savior. Once a Jew takes that plunge, he is cursed by the rabbis and called names like *meshummad* (traitor). Even Jewish atheists and agnostics shun him, cutting him off from ordinary Jewish fellowship.

Two full days went by, and the thought of smoking grass was as attractive as smoking a piece of rope. The Holy Spirit, whose other name is the Spirit of Truth, convicted my heart. I could no longer deny Him who had saved me. So I got down on my spiritual knees, thanked Him for who He was and what He'd done for me, then gave my life over to Him— gratefully—forever. In that instant, I passed from death into life. As John says, "And this is the testimony: that God has given us eternal life, and this life is in His Son. He who has the Son has life; he who does not have the Son of God does not have life" (1 John 5:11–12).

Now I had the Son and was born again as an acceptable member of God's family. My heart rejoiced in a new way and sang a new song to His glory and praise. All guilt had vanished. My conscience was as clear as a baby's. At last I'd come home to my Maker. But I still had a big problem— Juneau.

Little did I know the miracles the Holy Spirit was performing in her heart at *exactly the same time,* though her experience was totally unlike my conversion . . .

> *Though we read the Bible regularly and believed much of it, there were parts I dismissed as mere myths, well-meaning tales written by fervent writers. Talk about the blood of Christ seemed pure fantasy. I could not understand how someone could pay for another's sins. It made absolutely no sense. And for God to be a man did not jibe with my understanding of an all-powerful, omnipresent, all-knowing Being.*
>
> *One evening I was sitting in bed, reading a short description by Hal Lindsey of the death of Jesus. Suddenly, I felt as if I were there, and for the first time in my life I understood that Jesus is God and He suffered horribly on the cross for the sins of all the world—including mine.*
>
> *I realized this perfect, innocent Man had suffered the guilt of every sin that had ever been committed and would yet be done in the future. Worst of all, the Father could not be present with sin, and so He was gone during the time of His Son's ordeal. I sobbed and cried for His pain. Love for Him overflowed my heart. The Holy Spirit had moved my soul.*
>
> *The day after I accepted Christ as my Savior, I was amazed to find I now knew every word in the Bible was absolutely true. But I did not tell David. Not knowing that David was already a true Christian, I was afraid he might throw doubt on my discovery. Wouldn't he think it was just an emotional reaction if I couldn't think or speak about Jesus on the cross without weeping? But if I didn't speak of it, the furniture would have cried out. That very week, we confessed to each other that we were true Christians, born of the Spirit, confessing Jesus Christ as Lord and Savior. Oh, the miracle of the Holy Spirit, who worked on us in different ways to the same blessed end!*

Easter Friday was the darkest day for us now, as we relived the day He had done it all for love of us. That weekend we felt it would be good to fellowship with other Christians. Since Sunday was the traditional day for Christian worship, we would celebrate our Sabbath as always and go to a church service on Sunday.

On Easter Sunday 1984, we visited a little church just down the road from our house. The pastor did not preach the Easter message we needed to hear that day. We yearned to hear a retelling of the greatest miracle of all time, when Christ rose from the grave to bring hope to the world forever. That morning we had set our video recorder to tape another service being telecast from Ventura. Held at the local Seventh-day Adventist church, the service memorialized veterans of the Vietnam War, reconciling those who fought with native Vietnamese. As wounded veterans in uniform embraced Vietnamese members of the church, tears of joy flowed on the screen as well as in our watching eyes.

"I think they have services on the Sabbath," I said. "Maybe that would be the church for us."

We located an Adventist church in a nearby town, and the following Saturday we attended services. Following a violin duet, a small choir sang sweetly, then a lady played a hymn with bells, and the pastor preached a mellifluous sermon that went on just long enough not to be tiresome. As a worship experience it was pleasant enough, if not fiery, and on our way out we completed visitors' cards. That next Saturday, several older members of the congregation introduced themselves and invited us to lunch after services.

So began a ritual of Saturday morning churchgoing and afternoon lunches, with the same group of three elders and their wives. As new Christians, we hungered for spiritual information but though they were sweet and gentle-spirited, our new church friends never seemed willing to talk about God or His Word. That was when George Vandeman—host of television's "It Is Written" who attended our Thousand Oaks church—over a potluck lunch confided that they were praying the Holy Spirit to bring us in as members.

It was hinted that I might join their media ministry as a

writer. Vandeman urged us to attend an evening "Seminar for the End Times" that looked into the Bible and what Adventists believe, so we signed up. Held each Monday evening at the church, a typical session began with a video tape of Vandeman discussing Satan, rebellion, the mark of the Beast, and other subjects.

The presentation was slick, professional, and full of poetic generalities. Vandeman used the jump-around method of Bible texting. He had us code the special Bibles distributed the first night, and we'd go from a verse in Proverbs, coding it *SR* for Satan's rebellion, to another in Mark or Revelation where we'd dutifully ink in similar *SR*'s, without having the faintest idea of background or reason behind the analysis. The tape was followed by a forty-minute teaching session run by the pastor, Howard Welklin, and an architect named Ralph Arnold, who liked calling the twenty group members "my beloved" after the manner of the apostles.

Every time Juneau or I posed questions or challenged an interpretation, Welklin put us off. "You're jumping the gun a bit. We're going to cover that in a future session," he would say. Or "we've got too much to cover tonight and not enough time. Let's go into that some other time." Needless to say, the "right time" never arrived, and we had lots of unanswered questions rattling around in our heads and hearts.

Soon we got into the "gift of prophecy" and learned that Adventists believe the life and writings of Ellen G. White fulfill Revelation 12:17 and 19:10 concerning the remnant church of the last days. Since that didn't jibe with what we understood about Christian doctrine, we bought a set of White's books to find out what she—and therefore this church—teaches.

We found many of White's ideas troublesome—that America was the "image of the Beast" who would soon outlaw Saturday worship, that Christians who observed on Sunday had the mark of the Beast to condemn them in the last days, that God's covenant with Israel had been revoked and given to the new "spiritual Israelites" who accepted Christ and kept all God's commandments, especially the Sabbath day—which pretty much limited salvation to Adventists and a few Seventh-day Baptists. There were lots more rules about health, jewelry, wine, and food in White's books, prohibitions that make a total mockery of salvation through God's grace alone.

Early in the new year we joined a small study group held early Saturday mornings before services, run by the associate pastor, Ole Oleson. Like Welklin, Ole found lots of reasons to duck our questions. Though we were getting more serious Bible study at home alone, we found little to upset us at the church.

Until the day the Holy Spirit urged us to get baptized, just as Jesus had instructed. It was late spring, and right after our morning study, I told Ole we wanted to be baptized.

"Wonderful, wonderful," he beamed. "But I need to know what you understand of baptism?"

"It's a public acknowledgment that we've accepted Jesus as Lord and Savior," I said. "It means we're putting our lives completely in His hands and want our brothers and sisters in Christ to share in it. He told His disciples to go baptize people in the name of the Father, Son, and Holy Spirit. That's what we want to do."

"All right," Ole said. "But that's not all of it. I'll tell Howard about your request, and we'll get back to you."

The following Monday at the seminar, Pastor Welklin explained that baptism by Adventists means joining the Adventist church and accepting all the church's tenets. He gave us a card with twenty points of Adventist faith. Some described traditional Christian doctrine; others were more offbeat—for example their foot-washing ritual, or their teaching that the dead were "unconscious" and that wicked people were punished by obliteration, not eternal torment. Most troublesome, though, was their stress on obeying rules—especially the Seventh-day Sabbath—plus their emphasis on Ellen White as a bona fide prophet, in a class with Elijah and Isaiah.

One night as we were lying in bed, I raised the question of our baptism.

"I really want to get baptized," I said. "It's the right thing to do."

"But we have to join their church!" Juneau protested.

"So we join," I said. "We don't have to go along with all their rules."

"Yes we do. Yes we do!" she cried. "I don't want to spend my life feeling guilty. You don't understand, David, they're another cult. They have all these rules and regulations that cancel out the whole blessing of God's grace!"

Suddenly, Juneau began sobbing uncontrollably. Her reaction was so intense I was frightened and tried to console her.

"Look, I don't understand it exactly, but if it makes you that miserable, we'll just forget it."

It took us a long time to get to sleep after the emotional upheaval, but after that our spirits were calmed. Soon afterward I wrote a lengthy letter to the pastor explaining how our studies had led us to withdraw our request for baptism in their church. Pointing out the doctrines we saw as heretical, we felt their church was trying to earn salvation through rules. Concluding "So we hope you will understand why we shall not be attending services nor future classes, though we are grateful for the eighteen months of fellowship you shared with us," we sent copies to all those Adventists we'd come to know and love.

Not going to church left a gap in our lives, but we gained new purity of heart that inspired our home studies.

Fed up with churches, we vowed not to affiliate with any denomination. Instead we watched and supported those electronic ministers who spoke to our hearts, worshiped privately, and held our own home Bible studies. One Sunday Juneau suggested we sit in on a Bible class at the little Bible church down the street. We were directed to an over-forties group, which was led by television producer Michael Warren of "Happy Days." We found the class—as well as our classmates—absolutely charming, full of love and good humor. Most gratifying, though, was the teaching. Warren worked strictly from the text, and welcomed questions, challenges, and opinions from his students. This was a living fulfillment of Peter's admonition to "Be ready always to give to every man an answer" (1 Peter 3:15).

After three Sundays of classes, just as we were leaving for home, Gary Butler—a friendly fellow we'd come to know and love—suggested we try a service "just to see what's happening." So we did. And found an uncompromising pastor, Dave Gudgel, preaching the true Word of God, equally open to inquiry and ready to give an answer to every question.

It wasn't long before the Agoura Bible Fellowship became our own extended family, a body of believers who take God and His Word seriously enough to want to know all they can about it and Him. We asked Pastor Dave to baptize us, and though we were not yet members, he joyfully agreed. On Good Friday 1986, Juneau and I declared before man and God that Jesus Christ is our Lord, our God who died so we might live, and who rose from the grave to prove His dominion over life and death.

Two months later, we became members. Today Juneau and I sing in the choir, I serve on the deacon board, and she is on the church's design committee. More important, we know Christ, live from Him, and trust Him for our lives and happiness.

How can we be sure our faith in Christ is not just another false turning on the Sunshine Road? Or that biblical truth is not just one more cultic belief?

It's been four years now since we accepted Jesus as our Lord and Savior. In every spiritual trip we've ever taken, the process was identical. We'd start out full of high hopes and enthusiasm and go downhill from there. Soon the disenchantment would set in. We'd begin to notice the flaws, pierce through the phoniness, measure the unfulfilled promises, and feel the pain of a false faith agonizing our hearts.

Living through Jesus Christ, exactly the reverse is true. Day by day, week by week, month after month and year after year, our faith grows stronger. Our hearts are more filled with joy, our testing of Scripture only proves all the more that it is God's revealed Truth for all mankind. That's why Juneau and I had to tell our story of The Sunshine Road. If we didn't speak up, the rocks and trees would have shouted—for it is God's will that all His children return to His fold now, at this very special moment in history.

This is an extraordinary time we live in. A rising tide of New Age philosophy engulfs the world, with "spirit channelers," psychics, astrologers, cults, and outright Satanists growing bolder and spreading their beliefs with no outcry from governments or mass media.

New Age ideas are drawn from a wide range of religions and beliefs that oppose Judeo-Christianity—ancient paganism, Far Eastern faiths like Hinduism and Buddhism, modern psychology, Shamanism, humanism, and computer-age concepts. Many of these people sincerely believe in their doctrines and illusions. And they all share a contempt for the Word of God, especially when the Bible condemns their dangerous practices and warns of God's wrath against those who persist.

At the very same time, more people are being drawn to the truth of God's Word, just as Juneau and I were rescued by His ministering grace. Sides are being drawn, and there is no middle ground possible. Here are the stakes.

New Age believers are convinced that Christians, Jews, and others who put their faith in a personal God cannot inherit the coming age of peace and prosperity. By refusing to accept their own divinity, Christians and Jews are fated to stay at a lower level of consciousness. Therefore, believing Christians and Jews are a threat to their universal blessings of peace, happiness, and love that will arrive once the New Age appears.

Judeo-Christians, rooted in the entire Bible, stand firmly on God's promises and instruction. So many have already come true that people must be temporarily blinded and deaf not to see, hear, and open their hearts to their Maker who stands knocking at their door. God says—and Juneau and I know from hard experience—that calling on any supernatural power except the One who made heaven, earth, and everything in and on them is actually calling on the spirits of hell.

There is no common ground between the Christian who says, "The Lord, He is God," and Shirley MacLaine who says, "I am God."

We tried it both ways, so we know. Take it from a

brother and sister who've been there—The Lord is God. And His heart breaks to know you. As He said Himself in Deuteronomy 30:19: "I call heaven and earth as witnesses today against you, that I have set before you life and death, blessing and cursing; therefore choose life, that both you and your descendants may live."

◆

Which New Age Ideas Have Influenced You?

1. Do you know your astrological sign, and your astrological traits? Do you ever read astrology books or the astrology column in your morning newspaper?
2. Do you have living heroes who seem bigger than life? If so, do you tend to follow what they believe and model yourself on their example?
3. Do you believe you can join forces with other people to bring about world peace or an end to human suffering?
4. Are you attracted to philosophies or religious teachings that claim to be new, modern interpretations of what the Bible really means? Do you believe religious truth is progressing toward a higher understanding of who, or what, God really is?
5. Do you set goals for yourself, determining what you'll be doing, where you'll be living, and how rich you will be ten to twenty years from today?
6. Do you ever try to affect events or influence other people by visualizing the results you'd like?
7. Do you feel ancient Eastern religions, such as Hinduism, have something to teach us since they are older than the Bible?
8. Do you believe God resides in all created things, including trees, plants, water, earth, insects, animals, and humans?
9. Do you agree that modern science will eventually find the answers to all of man's problems, including cures for disease, short life spans, mental illnesses, and poverty?

10. Do you believe psychology holds the key to understanding all mental and emotional problems?
11. Do you feel there are planets more advanced than ours whose people may be visiting Earth?
12. Do you believe humankind is growing more advanced in every way through the ages?
13. Do you enjoy taking mind trips using impressionistic music, strobe lights, laser theater, color wheels, or environmental sound?
14. Do you consistently take part in hypnotic experiments, either with other people or by yourself?
15. Have you ever had the feeling that you have lived before?
16. Do you believe certain objects or materials are endowed with special powers to cure disease, see into the future, or bring good luck?
17. Do you depend upon people who claim to have the power to predict the future, read minds, recreate the past, or cure illness through psychic powers?
18. Do you use yoga stretching and positions as a form of exercise?
19. Do you play occult games for fun with friends, such as board games, Ouija boards, mind-reading cards, tarot cards, or ESP experiments?
20. Have you ever visited a psychic or fortune teller just for fun? Do you enjoy tuning in on psychics who appear on radio or television?
21. Do you feel you can gain peace of mind by meditating on a sound, a sacred word, or an inspirational picture?
22. Do you believe that "you are what you eat," that if you can only learn to eat right, then health and long life are assured?
23. Do you believe that there are many roads and ways to God?
24. Do you have a lucky number?

Glossary of New Age Words

agent—A person sending a telepathic message.

Akashic record—Imperishable records of every persons' every word, thought and deed inscribed in the earth or spirit realms.

Alpha—The physical body.

Ashram—A Hindu place of study under a guru.

astral body—A spiritual body inhabiting a physical body, capable of projection, and assumed at the death of the individual.

astral flight—Soul travel, particularly during sleep.

aura—Radiated glow or halo surrounding living beings.

automatic writing—Writing produced without conscious thought of a living person, through a spirit guide, by pencil or a typewriter.

Bhagavad Gita—Hindu sacred scripture.

Buddha—"The Enlightened One."

channeling—See "Trance channeling."

clairaudience—Ability to hear mentally without using the ears.

clairvoyance—Ability to see mentally without using the eyes, beyond ordinary time and space limits; also called "Second Sight."

control—The spirit that sends messages through a medium in trance.

deja vu—The feeling of having already experienced an event or place actually being encountered for the very first time.

discarnate—The soul or personality of a living creature who has died.

dowser—Sensitive using forked stick which points to hidden water, oil, buried money, lost articles, and people.

ectoplasm—A white substance pouring from a medium's body openings, supposedly denoting the presence of a disembodied spirit.

ESP—Extrasensory perception, encompassing paranormal abilities such as telepathy, precognition and clairvoyance.

ESP cards—Pack of twenty-five cards bearing five symbols, including stars, squares, circles, crosses and waves.

graphology—Character analysis and foretelling based on handwriting.

guru—Teacher or master.

ghost—A deceased person emotionally or tragically bound to a place.

harmonic convergence—Assembly of New Age meditators, gathered at the same propitious astrological time in different locations to bring in peace on earth and one-world government.

holistic health—Belief that the body is a blend of physical, mental, and spiritual forces, and that good health results from harmony of all three; uses macrobiotic diet, spirit healing, psychology, herbs, vitamins.

Kabala—Hebrew mystery lore based on mystical interpretation of the Bible; magical, occult practices stemming from the Middle Ages.

karma—Sanskrit for law of cause and effect; deeds good or bad from various lifetimes that will work out in this life or next.

Kirlian photography—A photographic process that measures living auras.

Kundalini—The elemental energy of the human body which, like a serpent, rests coiled at the base of the spine.

levitation—Raising of objects or people off the ground without using physical energy.

magic circle—Ring drawn by occultists to protect them from the spirits and demons they call up by incantations and rituals.

mandala—A design, usually concentric, that focuses attention to a single point.

mantra—A sacred word or phrase used repetitively to obtain peace, prosperity, and wisdom.

medium—A psychic or sensitive living person whose body is used as a vehicle for communicating with spirits.

metaphysics—The science of the supernatural.

New Age movement—Loose conglomeration of people, many of them "Yuppies" of the 1960s generation, who believe the world has entered the Aquarian age, when peace on earth and one-world government will rule. They see themselves as advanced in consciousness, rejecting Judeo-Christian values and the Bible in favor of Oriental philosophies and religion. Among them may be found environmentalists, nuclear freeze proponents, Marxist-socialist utopians, mind-control advocates, ESP cultists, spiritists, witchcraft practitioners, and others using magical rites.

Nirvana—Liberation from earthly things; paradise.

numerology—The analysis of hidden or prophetic meaning of numbers.

occultism—Belief in supernatural forces and beings.

om—A word symbolizing Brahma, the Creator God.

One Worlders—Those who advocate the abolition of nations, working to hand over power to a single-world government similar in structure to the present United Nations; offshoots of the United World Federalists founded in the 1930s.

Ouija board—Game designating all the letters of the alphabet plus numbers from 0 to 9 and "Yes/No." A sliding pointer (planchette) spells out words in answer to questions asked by players, supposedly by "spirits."

out-of-body experience—Leaving the physical body while at rest, asleep, near death, or temporarily dead.

pantheism—Doctrine that identifies God with the whole universe, every particle, tree, table, animal, and person being part of Him.

paranormal—Beyond or above normal human powers or senses.

parapsychology—Study of psychic phenomena using scientific methods.

pendulum—Heavy object on a string, used for dowsing.

pentagram—Five-pointed star used in magical ceremonies.

percipient—Person who receives telepathic messages.

poltergeist—German for a noisy, mischievous, destructive spirit.

precognition—Advance knowledge of future events.

Psi—Term used in place of *psychic* or *paraphysical;* ESP.

psychic energy—Extrasensory energy that enables people to do miracles.

psychic healer—A person who cures mental or physical illness from the cosmic energy emanating through the healer's hands.

psychoanalysis—Tracing mental and physical ills back to hurtful childhood experiences; based on Sigmund Freud's theories.

psychometry—Reading information from an object about events involving person who owns it, usually by handling it.

reincarnation—Belief that souls return again and again to a physical body to atone for past errors and work toward perfection.

retrocognition—Knowledge of past events learned paranormally.

seance—A gathering of people seeking communication with deceased loved ones or famous historical figures through a medium.

sensitive—A person who frequently demonstrates extrasensory gifts, such as clairvoyance, telepathy, or precognition.

shaman—A medicine man or witch doctor.

spirit control—A disembodied spirit who relays messages from dead people to the living through a trance medium.

spirit guide—A disembodied spirit who speaks or writes through a living person.

spiritualist—Person who believes in the ability to contact departed souls through a medium.

subject—Person used for experiments in ESP studies.

Sufism—Persian mystical religion based on Mohammedanism.

tarot cards—Deck of seventy-eight cards that supposedly reveal the secrets of man and the universe.

telekinesis—The ability to move physical objects by force of will or mental energy alone; also called psychokinesis.

telepathy—Communication between minds by extrasensory means.

tetragram—A magic diagram shaped as a four-pointed star.

third eye—Pineal gland, located at center of forehead above the nose; spiritual eye said to be the seat of visions and wisdom.

trance—A mental state resembling sleep during which the conscious mind rests while a spirit entity takes over the medium's body.

trance channeler—The newest term for "trance medium."

trumpet medium—A psychic or sensitive who brings forth "spirit voices" through a trumpet at seances.

UFO—Unidentified flying object; flying saucer.

Veda—The most ancient of the Hindu scriptures.

warlock—A wizard or sorcerer; a male witch.

yoga—A means to becoming united with the Supreme Being, or with the universal soul.

yogi—Someone who practices yoga.